D0264797

THE WESTMINSTER CONFESSION

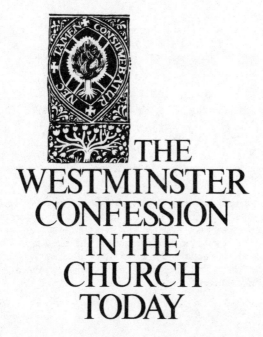

THE WESTMINSTER CONFESSION IN THE CHURCH TODAY

Papers prepared for the Church of Scotland
Panel on Doctrine

Edited by Alasdair I. C. Heron

THE SAINT ANDREW PRESS
EDINBURGH

First published in 1982 by
THE SAINT ANDREW PRESS
121 George Street, Edinburgh EH2 4YN

Copyright © The Saint Andrew Press, 1982

Reprinted 1982

ISBN 0 7152 0497 1

Printed in Great Britain by Bell and Bain Ltd., Glasgow

CONTENTS

FOREWORD

The Westminster Confession of Faith occupies an important place in the history and life of the Church of Scotland and of other churches in the Presbyterian family. In recent years, however, there has been renewed controversy on the status that ought to be accorded to it. This collection of papers does not seek to resolve that controversy, nor to pronounce upon it, but rather to provide relevant background information on some of the issues raised, some of the views held, and some of the solutions offered.

Since the working party of the Panel on Doctrine which is responsible for the preparation of this volume was set up to consider a remit from the General Assembly of the Church of Scotland, the Scottish debate was bound to be of primary concern. The topics discussed and the contributions received are, however, of interest far beyond the domestic ecclesiastical scene, and it is the hope of the Panel that many individuals and churches outwith Scotland will also find something of value in the papers presented here.

As so often in the past, the Panel is indebted to contributors from parishes and colleges who have given freely of their knowledge and time to accomplish a substantial piece of work. In addition, comments were sought for and most willingly given by scholars from other churches who have experience of a similar debate within their own tradition. To all our contributors I would express the Panel's sincere thanks.

Special mention must be made of the responsibility undertaken by Professor Alasdair Heron in editing this book. In so doing, he has added yet another valuable service to the many he has already done for the Panel and the Church.

IAN G. SCOTT
Convener of the Panel on Doctrine

INTRODUCTION

Revd Professor Alasdair I. C. Heron

The Westminster Confession is justly regarded as one of the most impressive of all the confessions framed by the Reformers or their successors in the sixteenth and seventeenth centuries. It has also been unusually widely influential, chiefly because of the special place given to it in the Church of Scotland and other Presbyterian Churches through the last three and a half centuries. Yet the status it has enjoyed has also provoked searching questions about the theological adequacy and continuing relevance of its teaching — questions which began to come to the surface in Scotland in the eighteenth century, grew acute in the nineteenth, and are still with us today.

The immediate occasion for the gathering of this collection of papers was the instruction given by the 1978 General Assembly of the Church of Scotland to its Panel on Doctrine to consider afresh the position of the Confession as the principal subordinate standard of the Church. In the background to that instruction lay the debate surrounding earlier proposals of the Panel — proposals which would have dispensed with the idea of a subordinate standard, treated the Confession as a historic document with a special place in the Presbyterian tradition, and substituted for it a statement of fundamental doctrines to be affirmed by ministers and elders on their ordination and admission to office. These proposals at the very last stage of the prescribed procedure failed to clear the final hurdle when the General Assembly of 1974 agreed by a majority to depart from the matter for the time being.

The working party which the Panel then set up in 1978 was aware of the continuing division of opinion within the Church.

1

Some feel that continued adherence to the Confession is a vital bulwark of the Church's faith, and indeed of its identity. Others are convinced that the qualifications with which the Confession is hedged about make the adherence required of ministers and elders a mere formality, largely meaningless and in practice ineffectual, and that the Church must express its doctrinal basis with greater definiteness than the Confession can enable. Others again recognise the ambiguity of the *status quo*, but see advantages in leaving matters as they are.

The working party was also conscious that for some ministers, many office-bearers, and the vast majority of members of the Church, the Confession is simply not a live issue at all — in part at least because of widespread unfamiliarity alike with the text of the document and with its history in the Church. This too inevitably hinders the Church from reaching a single mind on the issues posed by the Confession's official standing. After several initial discussions, it came to seem that the best service the working party could perform for the Panel and the Church at this stage was not to advance immediate proposals concerning the status of the Confession, but to try to make more widely available some essential information about it, and at the same time to offer a forum in which a range of views about the present position and possible ways forward might be canvassed.

This double aim determined the shape of the collection. The first two papers, by Professors McEwen and Cheyne, deal historically with the framing of the Confession and the role it has played in the Church through the last three and a half centuries. Then Dr Ferguson and Professor Torrance focus in more detail on the teaching of the Confession and the strengths and weaknesses of its theological scheme. Professor Lyall analyses the legal position, both in terms of Church law and of the State, and Mr Pettigrew explains the former Panel proposals and the discussion that surrounded them. Then follow five briefer papers describing how similar questions concerning the Confession have been tackled in countries other than Scotland. Finally, four ministers of the Church offer their own views on the attitude the Church should now adopt to the Confession. Some of the most important documents determining the present standing and interpretation of the Confession in the Church are given for convenience in an Appendix.

It will be apparent that not only the authors of the four final papers, but also those of the first six are not necessarily of one single opinion about the Confession and its future role in the Church. This was a conscious choice on the part of the working party which both selected the subjects and proposed the names of the contributors. If an amicable and brotherly resolution of the tensions which even today surround the Confession is to be reached at all, it must be through an open dialogue in which arguments and viewpoints are presented and tested. This is not to say that the Panel on Doctrine will not in the future come forward with specific recommendations in the light of these studies and subsequent developments; but the first need is for a clearing of the ground, for clarification of the past and present position, and for the objective evaluation of different possible ways forward.

The range of relevant issues raised in the different papers is a wide one; and if they are successful in stimulating further discussion in the Church, it may be expected that yet further facets of the matter will be disclosed. This is therefore not yet the place or time to attempt anything in the way of a comprehensive summing-up. Nor do I feel it would be appropriate for me to use this Introduction to argue for what happen to be my own opinions about the Confession. It may however be worth while to note some of the main questions which are raised in various forms in the different papers — questions which are directly relevant to any judgment about the future role of the Confession in the Church. Each of them could be debated at considerable length, but at this point it may be better simply to draw attention to them quite briefly.

How sound is the general teaching and tone of the Confession? How far is it time-conditioned, and how far might it still be seen as a Confession for today?

Does the Confession function effectively as the principal subordinate standard of the Church? What are the implications of the Declaratory Acts and the 'conscience clause'? Could it function more effectively — or, alternatively, is a principal subordinate standard necessary at all?

How far is the Church at liberty to modify the standing of the Confession? What consequences for the Church's own identity might follow?

What practical alternatives might there be to the present position? What grounds might be advanced for preferring them? Or is the present position essentially satisfactory?

The list could be drawn out further; but these, I would suggest, are the main issues that the Church needs to face. It would be a great pity if the debate should simply polarise between those who would make a shibboleth of the Confession and those who would make a shibboleth of disposing of it; it would also be regrettable if the Church preferred in effect to drift onward without openly facing the issues and becoming clear as to its real convictions.

Over and above the immediate goal of helping to inform current discussion in the Church, it is also our hope that these papers may prove of interest and use to those who are concerned to study this central strand in our Scottish Presbyterian history. Dr Murray in his contribution observes that when he was a Divinity student in Edinburgh in the late 1960s, virtually no attention was given in any of the courses he attended to the Confession and its theology. More recent years have brought a significant change, and, in more than one of our Divinity Faculties, courses are now offered which give special place to the Scottish Church and to Scottish theology, including the teaching and influence of the Confession. Whether or not it remains the Church's principal subordinate standard, such study will surely deserve to remain an important element in the engagement of our students with their own history. Even if the work of the Westminster divines should at last be relegated, like the *Scots Confession*, to the status of an honoured historical document, we shall still do well to apply to it what the late Professor G. D. Henderson wrote of the *Scots Confession*:

There is no thought of renewing the Covenants today, and similarly there is no thought of returning to the use of the *Scots Confession*. Both were essentially temporary in character, but they mark experiences in the spiritual history of our race which have helped to make it what it is. We shall not pass that way again, whatever

changes may befall us, but we have in fact passed that way; and we
shall be none the less able to help our own generation to express its
spiritual convictions, if we honour the memory and appreciate the
effort of those who ... made such splendid acknowledgment ... of
the Sovereignty of God. ...[1]

Finally I should like to express the warm appreciation of the
working party for the generous willingness of the contributors to
co-operate in this task, and to add an editor's personal thanks for
the very considerable amount of work which these papers
represent. May they prove both informative and helpful to the
Church as it considers afresh its relation to the standard which
has so long been given primary place in its formularies.

1. G. D. Henderson, *The Burning Bush*. Edinburgh: The Saint Andrew Press,
1957, p. 41.

HOW THE CONFESSION CAME TO BE WRITTEN

Revd Professor James S. McEwen

Reformation Confessions in Scotland

Three Confessions current in Scotland during the Reformation period may be singled out for particular attention:

(*a*) *Patrick's Places.* This was the work of Patrick Hamilton the martyr, composed in Latin at Marburg University in 1526 and subsequently translated into Scots/English. Completely Lutheran in outlook, it is a compact and persuasive statement of evangelical truth, and was highly valued by those who cared for Reform.

(*b*) *The First Helvetic Confession* — the agreed statement of all the Evangelical Swiss Cantons. About 1540 Wishart the martyr, while a refugee in Switzerland, translated the Confession into English. He also translated the Zurich Communion-office, and the Swiss Confession and the Zurich Communion-office served to define Reformed Church membership in Scotland prior to 1560.

(*c*) *The Scots Confession, 1560.* Prepared in four days by Knox and his friends when Parliament demanded of them a statement of the Reformed Faith which should be established in Scotland. This is a moderately Calvinist document, not without occasional Lutheran overtones.

We thus realise that Scotland possessed three Reformation confessions, reflecting different aspects of the Continental Reformation, and associated with each of her leading Reformers; and the first and last of them are wholly the work of Scotsmen.

It is a curious and rather sad fact that all three of these confessions have passed into virtual oblivion; and our present standard — the Westminster Confession — has no connection with these historic statements of the Scottish Reformation.

Reformation Confessions in England

In England, from the time of the Reformation onwards, the various forms of the Articles of the Church of England have dominated the confessional scene. First came the brief Articles of 1536 and 1538 reflecting the 'Reformation' as sanctioned by Henry VIII. Both sets of Articles are Lutheran and rest on the Augsburg Confession. The Forty-two Articles of Edward VI move considerably in the Swiss direction. The Thirty-nine Articles of Elizabeth are an amalgam of moderate Lutheranism and moderate Calvinism. The Thirty-nine Articles have remained dominant in England except during the brief Westminster interlude; and they have spread wherever Anglicanism has gone throughout the world.

Of more immediate importance, however, for a study of the Westminster Confession were Archbishop Ussher's Irish Articles of 1615 — fairly strongly Calvinist in tone, and quite clearly constituting the pattern upon which the Westminster Confession was modelled, mainly as regards form, but to some extent also in content. Ussher was nominated as a member of the Assembly; he does not appear ever to have attended, but his Articles exercised great influence.

Why the Scots permanently abandoned their rich confessional heritage, and why the English temporarily departed from the Thirty-nine Articles, is the question that now confronts us. To understand this we must take a rapid glance at historical events in both countries from the Union of the Crowns to the outbreak of the Civil War.

1. Events in Scotland, 1603 to 1640
When Charles I came to the throne in 1625 he inherited from his father an explosive situation. James VI had long detested Scottish Presbyterianism which appeared to him to be incompatible with royal authority. As king of the Scots he had

struggled against it with limited success, but from the remote security of the English throne he set himself to break the power of the Scottish Church and to reshape it after the Anglican model which he found to be entirely in keeping with his personal views on the divine right of kings in Church and State. He drove the Presbyterian leaders into banishment, bullied and gagged the General Assembly, and gradually moved the 'Parliamentary Bishops' he had appointed in 1600 into full episcopal status with all the blessings of Anglican consecration.

It would have been well for James and still better for his unhappy son if he had stopped at that point. He had secured the essentials of Scottish Episcopacy with little sign of effective opposition. Some ministers were disgruntled, but the familiar worship of the Scottish Church continued unaltered, and so long as that was so the mass of Church members were unaware of any serious danger to the Kirk. James, however, was not content to stop short of complete assimilation of the Scottish Church to the Anglican model. His next step was therefore to meddle with worship, thereby forcing his religious activities directly upon the attention of the Scottish people. By the Five Articles of Perth in 1618 he sought to enforce such Anglican practices as kneeling at Communion, episcopal confirmation, the observance of certain festivals, and private baptism and communion. The changes were comparatively small, but each challenged the Reformed pattern of worship established by Knox, and there was widespread disobedience to the new regulations.

James was enraged, and determined to scourge Scotland, ministers and people, into obedience. Easter day 1625 was fixed on as the final day of testing. All the new ceremonies were to be fully enforced and dire penalties were to be exacted for any refusal to conform. James had all his plans laid to deal with the recalcitrant, but a few days before the fateful date he died leaving his son to deal with an irritated, resentful and suspicious nation. It was a perilous legacy, and Charles altogether lacked the capacity to handle the situation — or even to understand what it was.

Charles was a well-meaning and reasonably pious man, but stupidly obstinate and pathologically devious. He had the misfortune to inherit in full measure his father's belief in the divine right of kings, and the still greater misfortune of inheriting his father's favourite religious adviser, William Laud, whom he advanced to the post of Archbishop of Canterbury and loaded with civic appointments as well. Laud hated Calvinism, rejected the main Reformation doctrines, and laboured to bring back the old Catholic forms of worship. His crypto-Catholicism endeared him to Charles who was much under the influence of his own Roman Catholic wife.

Charles's first actions in Scotland were characteristically well-meaning, but foreseeably disastrous for himself. He attempted to claw back, for the benefit of the now-episcopal Church of Scotland, some of the wealth that the nobility had pilfered from the Church at the time of the Reformation, and in this project he was naturally eagerly supported by the Scottish bishops. This set the Scottish nobility bitterly against the crown and the bishops, and convinced them that Presbyterianism would be a less expensive form of religion — which opened the way for the alliance of nobility and commons against crown and bishops, which ushered in the Wars of the Covenant.

Charles took a further fatal step when he paid his first royal visit to Scotland in 1633 bringing Laud with him. Laud and his master were shocked by the bareness of Scottish worship and returned to London determined to give the Scots something better — whether they liked it or not. In 1636, therefore, the king appointed nineteen canons by Royal warrant, for the better ordering of worship in Scotland. Knox's Liturgy was abolished, use of the English Prayer Book enjoined, extempore prayer prohibited, the eldership and all Presbyterian courts tacitly assumed to be abolished, and excommunication enacted for any denial of the royal supremacy over the Scottish Church. In the following year 'Laud's Liturgy' was substituted in Scotland for the English Prayer Book, and Sunday 23rd July 1637 was fixed as the date of its introduction.

When the Scots examined the Liturgy they concluded that it contained stronger romanizing tendencies than they were prepared to tolerate, and that the time had come to resist royal meddling with the Scottish Kirk. The date set by the king for the introduction of the new Liturgy turned out instead to be a day of riot and protest which began quite spontaneously, but was not allowed to remain unorganized. Thirty of the leading members of the already disaffected nobility immediately stepped forward to add force to the nascent rebellion, and a powerful committee of nobles, lairds, burgesses and churchmen was set up to formulate and prosecute whatever course of action might be deemed necessary. Charles's inept attempts to split the committee by playing on divisive interests among the various classes involved, led to the prompt signing of the National Covenant which pledged the signatories, and indeed the whole nation, in a binding oath before God, to stand together in defence of the Reformed Faith and of Presbyterian Church government. The Covenant makes it clear that there is no intention of overthrowing the monarchy. It pledges full loyalty to Charles if he will consent to respect the religion, liberties and laws of Scotland. In other words, it demands constitutional monarchy and rejects Charles's cherished doctrine of the Divine Right of Kings.

Charles decided to put down the protest by force; but to do this he required to raise an army and the money to pay for it. Meantime he had to temporize. Reluctantly he allowed 'a free General Assembly' to meet in Glasgow in November 1638, which immediately took the bit between its teeth, and in outright defiance of royal authority abolished episcopacy, deposed the bishops, and restored the Kirk to full Presbyterianism. Furious, Charles took the field against the Scots, but was dismayed to discover a vastly superior Covenanting army waiting for him. Once again he had to temporize, promising to regard the authority of the General Assembly as final in religious matters, and that of the Scottish Parliament in matters civil.

By the late summer of 1640 Charles had wrung sufficient money by forced loans from the wealthier citizens of London to pay for another army — though he had to resort to press-gang methods to enlist the troops. Grumbling and discontented, the royal army straggled north to Newcastle; but a powerful Covenanting army swept south across the Border, brushed the royal army aside, and occupied Newcastle and Durham. For a year the army of the Covenant held the whole of the North of England, while Scottish negotiators went down to London and wrung from the king every concession that they demanded.

The presence in England of the Scottish army of occupation forced Charles to summon the English Parliament, and in November 1640 the Long Parliament began its work of slashing down royal authority and demolishing the king's most devoted ally — the episcopate.

2. Developments in England

The calling of the Long Parliament leads directly into the work of the Westminster Assembly, and our interest therefore now moves to events in England. A brief backward glance will better enable us to grasp the significance of these events.

From the days of Elizabeth the Puritans had constituted a discontented element in the English religious scene. Elizabeth had deliberately fixed on a religious settlement that would content the majority of Englishmen — her celebrated middle way — but with a clear enough slant away from Calvinism for which, as a Tudor despot, she had no liking. The Puritan leaders had been deeply influenced by Calvinism during their exile on the Continent in Mary's reign. Now back in England, they objected to what they regarded as lingering elements of Popish superstition in the Elizabethan Church and Prayer Book. Many of them went so far as to reject episcopacy and to advocate the substitution of a Presbyterian polity.

Elizabeth tolerated them just as long as she required their support against the discontented northern Catholics: when that menace was removed she turned upon the Puritans and sought to whip them also into line.

From about 1570 small groups of Puritans began to quit the established Church and set up congregations in which they instituted what they regarded as Scriptural worship and government. Almost of necessity these isolated congregations abandoned the idea of Presbyterianism and became more or less Congregational in polity. Elizabeth treated these separatists with ruthless cruelty, and this sowed in their minds seeds of bitterness — not only against the established Church, but also against the Presbyterian Puritans who, instead of going out into the wilderness and sharing the suffering of their separatist brethren, comfortably waited within the establishment in hope of a Presbyterian paradise when the king of Presbyterian Scotland should succeed Elizabeth.

Some of the separatist groups in exile on the Continent came in contact with the Mennonites and accepted their Baptist faith and practice. Between 1610 and 1620 Baptist congregations were multiplying in England, and a new wave of Congregationalism arose, so that the left wing of English Puritanism now contained Congregationalists, Baptists, and other separatists.

King James proved a bitter disappointment to the English Presbyterian Puritans. Before his accession to the throne he became aware that the English bishops, troubled by the rising tide of Puritanism, looked sourly on the prospect of a Presbyterian king. He accordingly dropped the hint that if they supported his accession they could count on his unbending hostility to both Presbyterianism and Puritanism. He was as bad as his word. At the Hampton Court Conference in 1604, called to consider Puritan requests for the reform of the English Church, James made his uncompromising opposition to Puritanism plain. 'I will have one doctrine, one discipline, one religion, in substance and in ceremony,' he declared: 'And I will make them conform, or I will harry them out of the land.'

Here then, at the start of his reign, began the fateful alliance of Church and king which polarized the country into a Royalist Episcopal party on the one side, and a Parliamentary and Puritan party on the other. The king's contempt for Parliament, and Parliament's suspicion of the king's foreign policy, led to increasing friction between Crown and Commons, while the bishops' enthusiastic support of the Crown produced growing anti-episcopal feeling in the Commons, which became increasingly Puritan in sympathy and composition.

Under King Charles, who altogether lacked his father's modicum of statesmanship, the polarization rapidly became more intense. Arbitrary taxation and arbitrary imprisonment by royal authority exasperated Parliament, and when Charles gagged all protest by suspending Parliament for a decade, relations between Crown and Parliament were damaged beyond repair.

Charles's promotion of the Anglo-Catholic and bitter anti-Puritan William Laud to be Archbishop of Canterbury, and personal friend and adviser to the king, ensured that relations between Parliament and the Church would be as severely damaged. Laud carried on a running persecution of the Puritans which did not stop short of brutalities like nose-slitting and ear-cropping; and since Puritanism was now very strongly represented in the Commons, a day of sore reckoning between Parliament and the Church became inevitable.

That day drew close, as we have seen, when the Scottish Covenanting army occupied the North of England and forced Charles to call the Long Parliament in November 1640 — a

Parliament in which the Presbyterian Puritans held the effective majority. Laud was hustled to the Tower, and when Charles attempted to use force against the Parliamentary leaders, the result was civil war.

It now became necessary for Parliament to bid for Scottish military support, and a delegation went to Edinburgh to seek a military league between the two kingdoms. The Scots, however, demanded more than a military league: they wanted the pledge of a religious settlement as well. For too long Presbyterianism, both in Scotland and England, had suffered under Episcopalian attack, and now the Scots saw a great opportunity of eliminating that menace permanently. In place of the Stuart aim of universal episcopacy, let England now join with Scotland in a religious Covenant to make the British Isles Presbyterian.

After some hesitation the English Parliament agreed, and the two nations entered into the Solemn League and Covenant — a military alliance conjoined with a solemn religious undertaking. On the religious side, the signatories bound themselves to seek 'conjunction and uniformity in Religion, Confession of Faith, Form of Church Government, Directory of Worship ... according to the Word of God and the example of the best Reformed Churches.' The Solemn League and Covenant thus directly implied the work of the Westminster Assembly.

The Westminster Assembly

The English Parliament had begun to clear the ground for religious reform even before the ratification of the Solemn League and Covenant in the autumn of 1643. Already in the spring they had passed an act which resulted in the abolition of episcopacy before the end of the year; and in July they set up the Westminster Assembly to advise Parliament on what should be put in its place. The Assembly consisted of 121 ministers selected by Parliament, and thirty laymen from Parliament. In its composition the Assembly accurately matched the religious complexion of the Parliament that appointed it: it contained a small number of Congregationalists and Episcopalians, but the great majority were Presbyterian Puritans. An invitation was extended to the Scots to appoint assessors to the Assembly with the right to debate but not to vote, and a small but influential delegation headed by Alexander Henderson joined the Assembly, where the Scots exercised great influence as experts in the Presbyterian system which England was now considering.

It is of some importance to realise that the Westminster Assembly was in no sense an independent religious body, and that it had no authority whatever to enact anything. It was the creation and instrument of Parliament, and the Parliamentary ordinance that set it up took pains to make that clear. The Assembly was instructed that it should consider those matters alone which Parliament should refer to it and no others, and 'this ordinance ... shall not give unto the persons aforesaid ... nor shall they in this Assembly assume to exercise, any jurisdiction, power, or authority ecclesiastical whatsoever ...'. The Assembly was simply an advisory body or committee created by Parliament and all its recommendations were laid before Parliament, debated, amended, or rejected by Parliament, or — where Parliament saw fit — accepted and enacted by Parliament. In all this, Parliament displayed its Erastian determination to be the final religious authority in the land — a determination that boded ill for any chance of establishing full-fledged Presbyterianism in England.

The most pressing duty of the Assembly at first was the preparation of a Directory of Public Worship to replace the English Book of Common Prayer, which Parliament had resolved to set aside. Even this modest task was not achieved without considerable trouble, for the extremer Puritans objected not only to the old Prayer Book, but to any authoritative directions at all concerning worship which might hamper the free leading of the Spirit. By January 1645, however, the Directory received Parliamentary sanction, and very shortly afterwards was accepted by the General Assembly and by Parliament in Scotland.

The large task of creating a Confession of Faith and two teaching catechisms naturally consumed much time, but the most exacting and troublesome matter was the preparation of a scheme of Church government for the English Church. The Scots assumed that the new Church should be fully Presbyterian: did not the Solemn League and Covenant so stipulate? The English Parliament professed not to be convinced that this was exactly what was stipulated. The truth was that they were reluctant to set up in England anything that in any way resembled the forceful autonomy of Scottish Presbyterianism. What government in its senses would create such a rod to belabour its own back? Whatever Church was set up in England must be firmly under Parliamentary control.

The Congregationalists and Baptists were, of course, resolutely opposed to a Presbyterian settlement. Not only did they question whether its centralised form of government was Scriptural, but they feared — not unjustifiably — that it would turn out to be fully as oppressive as Episcopacy had been. The sects had been given short shrift in Presbyterian Scotland: what hope would they have of better treatment in a Presbyterian England?

History does not stand still; and while these matters were being thrashed out in the Assembly and in Parliament, the Civil War continued and gradually brought about a situation in which the ground was cut from beneath the feet of the Presbyterian Puritans in Parliament, and their political ascendancy was destroyed. The architect of this situation was Oliver Cromwell, the Independent. His sympathies were Congregational in the main, but he extended a large benevolence to all sects provided they had no aspirations towards becoming exclusive national establishments. His phenomenal military successes made him increasingly a man to be reckoned with, and his highly efficient army was predominantly Independent in religious outlook. Thus the Presbyterian Parliament was served by a general and an army of Congregationalists, Baptists, and a variety of 'sectaries' who could not be expected to look with favour on the setting up of a Presbyterian Establishment exercising a Presbyterian discipline, with all that that implied. Parliament began to look over its shoulder with apprehensive eyes at its own army, and decided that it would not be prudent to proceed with the implementation of even that measure of Presbyterianism it had already sanctioned — let alone with its full establishment.

This failure to implement the terms of the Solemn League and Covenant angered the Scots who now staged a half-hearted adventure on the king's behalf. Cromwell gleefully cut them to pieces at Preston in 1648 and put Scotland under military occupation. Then, having smashed the military power of foreign Presbyterianism, he turned south to deal with the weaker home-grown variety. By 'Pride's Purge' in December of that same year, he chased the Presbyterians out of Parliament, leaving less than a hundred members to do exactly what the Independent army told them. In the following month they executed Charles, so that Independency was secured against any attack by either Presbyterianism or Episcopacy.

So ended the great Presbyterian adventure in England — destroyed not by the Goliath of Episcopacy but by the upstart little David of Independency. Presbyterianism now retreated north of the Tweed, and what remained of it in England dwindled to but a small remnant.

The Westminster documents obviously had relatively small importance in England after the collapse of Presbyterian Puritanism; but the Scottish General Assembly, in high hope and expectation of one Presbyterian Church of the British Isles, had already hastened to lay aside its Knoxian Liturgy and Creed in favour of the new Westminster standards, and continued to adhere to them even after the English collapse. It is thus a curious fact that Scottish Presbyterian standards in worship, faith, and even psalmody, are those that were authorised by a somewhat Erastian English Parliament in the mid-seventeenth century.

Even in Scotland, however, it seemed for a time that the Westminster Confession would pass into oblivion, for the end of the Commonwealth saw the restoration of Episcopacy under Charles II and the abolition of the Confession and the Catechisms by the infamous Rescissory Act.

With the landing of William of Orange in 1688, however, this Second Episcopacy came to an undistinguished end and Presbyterianism was finally restored. Parliament did not, however, restore all the Westminster standards to the Scottish statute book: indeed, it re-enacted only one of them — the Westminster Confession of Faith. This was not due to any hostility to them on the part of Parliament. It was simply pressure of business and shortage of time, and perhaps a measure of laziness, that moved Parliament to re-establish Presbyterianism by the simpler method of replacing on the Statute Book its own Act of 1592 in which it had established full 'Melvillian' Presbyterianism, with the sole variation of the Westminster in place of the Scots Confession. It was left to the General Assembly to do what it liked about the other Westminster standards.

THE PLACE OF THE CONFESSION THROUGH THREE CENTURIES

Revd Professor Alexander C. Cheyne

Not until nearly a century after the Reformation did the Church of Scotland acquire what is now officially described, in the language of the 1929 Act of Union, as its 'principal subordinate standard'. Until then, the doctrinal rallying-point of Reformed churchmen north of the Border had been the Scots Confession of Knox and his colleagues, described at its adoption by Parliament in 1560 as 'The Confession of Faith professed and believed by the Protestants within the realm of Scotland ... and by the Estates thereof ratified and approved as wholesome and sound doctrine, grounded upon the infallible truth of God's Word.' In 1647, however, the tides of Puritan revolution bore the recently completed Westminster Confession north to Edinburgh, and the General Assembly of that year gave their approval to it as 'most orthodox, and grounded upon the Word of God'. Two years later, all ministers were required positively to further its teaching; and at the same time the support of the ecclesiastical authorities was given additional weight by the ratification and approval of the Estates of Parliament.

The Confession had thus been well and truly launched upon its long career as a shaping influence in the life of both Church and nation, and the distresses occasioned by the Cromwellian occupation and the return of the Stuarts constituted only a brief interlude in the story of its rise to dominance. It regained favour in 1690 at the same time as the Revolution Settlement brought Presbyterianism back to power. But events soon showed that its rôle in the new epoch was to be subtly different from what it had been in earlier days. It continued, of course, to serve as a deeply-

17

valued affirmation of faith: in the words of the Act of Establishment, as 'the public and avowed Confession of this Church containing the sum and substance of the faith of the Reformed Church'. At the same time, however, it came to be used more and more as a weapon in the ecclesiastical power game (against Episcopalians) and as a touchstone of political reliability (against Jacobites).

The stages in what proved to be a fateful process may be briefly indicated. In October 1690, the restored General Assembly ordained that 'For retaining soundness and unity of doctrine, it is judged necessary that all probationers licensed to preach, all entrants into the ministry, and all other ministers and elders received into communion with us in Church government, be obliged to subscribe their approbation of the Confession of Faith.' In 1693, Parliament's controversial Act for Settling the Peace and Quiet of the Church gave state backing to use of the Confession as a test by requiring that 'no person be admitted, or continued for hereafter, to be a minister or preacher within this Church, unless that he do also subscribe the Confession of Faith ... declaring the same to be the confession of his faith, and that he owns the doctrine therein contained to be the true doctrine which he will constantly adhere to.' In 1694, the Assembly followed the politicians' lead with a formula of adherence to the Confession, which was to be signed by 'such of the late conforming ministers' (i.e., one-time compliers with the pre-Revolution Episcopalian régime) 'as were desirous of reception into the Kirk'; and in 1700 it enacted that '*all* ministers and ruling elders belonging to this National Church subscribe the Confession of Faith as the confession of their faith'. Subsequent Assembly legislation extended this requirement to further classes — commissioners to the Assembly, for example, in 1704, and licentiates in 1705.

But it was in 1711 that the coping stones were placed upon the edifice of enforced conformity. Not content with an 'Act for preserving Purity of Doctrine' (passed the previous year) which forbade the uttering of 'any opinions contrary to any head or article of the said Confession and Catechisms', the General Assembly now drew up certain questions, together with a formula of subscription, to be tendered to all the Church's servants at licensing, ordination, and induction. The second of the questions to be put to ministers at their ordination ran as follows: 'Do you sincerely own and believe the whole doctrine contained in the Confession of Faith ... to be founded upon the Word of God; and do you acknowledge the same as the confession of your faith; and will you firmly and constantly adhere thereto, and, to the utmost of your power, assert, maintain, and defend the same?' And the formula, to be subscribed by licentiates and ordained men alike, only clarified the extensiveness of the required commitment: 'I do hereby declare, that I do sincerely own and believe the whole doctrine contained in the Confession of Faith ... to be the truths of God, and I do own the same as the confession of my faith ... which doctrine ... I am persuaded [is] founded upon the Word of God, and agreeable thereto. And I promise that, through the grace of God, I shall constantly and firmly adhere to the same, and to the utmost of my power shall in my station assert, maintain and defend the said doctrine.... And I promise that I shall follow no divisive course from the present establishment in this Church, renouncing all doctrines, tenets and opinions whatsoever, contrary to or inconsistent with the said doctrine.'

The greatly increased rigour of these terms of subscription was almost certainly connected with the religious and political uncertainties of the later years of Queen Anne's reign. No sooner had the Union of the Parliaments of England and Scotland been consummated in 1707, than resurgent English Toryism showed itself intent upon the restoring of Episcopalian fortunes in Scotland as a step towards the destruction, or at least the reconstruction, of the Revolution Settlement throughout Great Britain. Scottish Presbyterianism — soon to be shaken by the Toleration and Patronage Acts, the one conceivably undermining its disciplinary system, the other undeniably interfering with its method of ministerial appointments — felt threatened and insecure. It reacted with measures which, though no doubt harsh and restrictive, are at least understandable in the circumstances. What *is* surprising, however, and also highly significant, is that although the worst forebodings of the period were not realised, and although the threat to the Revolution Settlement from Episcopalians and Jacobites gradually receded, the obligations concerning the Confession of Faith which had been imposed upon Scottish churchmen at the beginning of the eighteenth century continued to be binding at its close.

For a time at least they were not resented, though even as early as 1719 William Dunlop's *The Uses of Creeds and Confessions* opened with an admission that Confessions were now 'generally decried' and 'of late years not only undervalued as mean and useless, but exclaimed against as unjust, arbitrary, and inconsistent in their frame and tendency with the liberty of mankind'. A new attitude became evident, however, as the Kirk fell under the rule of the Moderates. One of their great enemies, John Witherspoon, declared in his *Ecclesiastical Characteristics* (published in 1753) that, 'It is a necessary part of the character of a Moderate man never to speak of the Confession but with a sneer; to give sly hints that he does not thoroughly believe it; and to make the word orthodoxy a term of contempt and reproach.' The accusation seemed to be borne out by several incidents during the 1760s and 1770s, the Moderates' hey-day. In 1767, the Reverend Alexander Ferguson of Kilwinning published an article in the *Scots Magazine* which expressed indifference to some of the central doctrines of Calvinistic orthodoxy, as contained in the Confession of Faith; and succeeding volumes of the same journal included correspondence which gave him some support. (The charges of heresy brought against him were, revealingly, dismissed by his Moderate-minded presbytery.) In 1771, a vigorous tract on the same subject, *The Religious Establishment in Scotland examined upon Protestant Principles*, subjected creeds and credal subscription to trenchant criticism. And we have it on the authority of the respected Sir Henry Moncreiff that Principal Robertson's retirement from the Moderate leadership in 1780 was precipitated by his embarrassment at 'the scheme into which many of his friends entered zealously for abolishing subscription to the Confession of Faith and Formula'. Even as late as 1786, Evangelicals both inside and outside the Establishment were outraged when the church courts accepted the explanations and apologies of the Reverend William McGill of Ayr, whose *A Practical Essay on the Death of Christ* had obviously diverged from Westminster orthodoxy.

The tepid or even critical attitude to the Confession which had characterised the Robertsonian epoch did not long survive the passing of Moderatism's greatest leader. Scarcely had the Principal bowed himself out (predicting, incidentally, that credal subscription would become 'the chief controversy of the next generation'), than the religious scene was entirely altered by the French Revolution and the conservative reaction precipitated by it throughout Great Britain; and soon both parties in the Church seemed to be vying with each other in professions of loyalty to the Westminster faith. Of Principal Hill, a Moderate but the most eminent theological teacher of his age, even Thomas Chalmers bore witness that his orthodoxy was 'formed in conformity to the Standards'; and the same could probably have been said about the vast majority of early nineteenth-century Moderates. As for the Evangelicals, their devotion to the Confession was unimpeachable: it was, indeed, one of the most obvious of the enthusiasms which they carried into the Free Church in 1843, helping to establish that body's reputation for rigid, not to say immobile, orthodoxy during the first decades of its existence. Conformity — sometimes reluctant, more often eager and whole-hearted — seemed to be the order of the day.

On the other hand, it has to be admitted that the new century had hardly begun when the hitherto almost unbroken facade of traditional orthodoxy began to show the first signs of crumbling. The Seceders, on some of whom 'new light' had dawned concerning the Confession's teaching about Church–State relations, appealed from the pronouncements of Westminster to Scripture itself and boldly testified that, 'As no human composure, however excellent and well-expressed, can be supposed to contain a full and comprehensive view of divine truth; so we are not precluded from embracing, upon due deliberation, any further light which may afterwards arise from the Word of God about any article of divine truth.' Edward Irving expressed a preference for the Scots Confession, which he considered a more admirable — perhaps because more militant? — document. John Macleod Campbell, speaking before the Synod of Glasgow while on trial for heresy, underlined the fact that for him the Confession of Faith was a truly *subordinate* standard, and declared: 'When the Church says to both ministers and people, "This is my Confession of Faith: if anything in it appear to you inconsistent with the Word of God, I am prepared to go with you to the Word of God to settle the matter", then does the Church speak according to her place. But if instead of this she says, "This I have fixed to be the meaning of the Word of God, and you cannot take any other meaning without being excluded from my communion; and to

entitle me so to exclude you I do not need to prove to you that
what you hold and teach is contrary to my Confession of Faith";
I say, if the Church of Christ use this language she no longer
remembers her place as a Church.' And James Morrison, on trial
before the Secession Church only a few years later, spoke to like
effect. All this between 1804 and 1841!

The first half of the nineteenth century nevertheless saw no
really substantial changes in Scotland's relationship either to
Westminster Calvinism in general or to the Confession in
particular — not, at any rate, if by that we mean changes which
affected large numbers of people and found unambiguous
expression in official church pronouncements. (It is arguable that
the Standards of the United Presbyterian Church indicate a
falling-away from the Westminster norm of earlier Secession
testimonies; but if they do it seems to have been an unconscious
departure.) All we can report are a few premonitory tremors
heralding the earthquake to come, no more; and even those
persons who occasionally felt moved to express their disquiet at
one aspect or another of the reigning theology, or at its
imposition upon ministers and office-bearers, did so in the most
hesitant and deferential manner. In 1850, it is true, a public
lecture at New College, Edinburgh by Professor James Buchanan
admitted the existence of a growing unease with all dogmatic,
confessional statements, and referred to current descriptions of
theology's technical terms as 'mere scholastic subtleties — the
remnants of a darker age, when the human mind was cramped
and fettered by bandages of its own fabrication'. But of course
Buchanan did not share the unease which he reported; and it
must be remembered that he and those who thought like him had
a virtual monopoly of all the positions of power and influence in
the Churches. (Almost the only exception was John Tulloch, who
went to St Mary's College, St Andrews, in 1854; and quite a few
years were to pass before the young professor carried much
weight.)

Even in the 1860s and 1870s, the weight of numbers in every
Presbyterian communion was still very much on the conservative
side, theologically speaking. The Moderator of the Auld Kirk
General Assembly in 1866 reminded the fathers and brethren that
'Our Confession, submitted to the Estates of Parliament, was
accepted as the truth of God; and the Church was ... not free at

any time to modify, alter, or depart from it, nor to hold the truth of any of its doctrines an open question' — though it is interesting that his statement provoked seventy ministers, under Tulloch's leadership, to protest that 'the old relation of our Church to the Confession cannot continue'. There is also general agreement that the 'Constitutionalist' opposition to union with the United Presbyterians which almost tore the Free Church asunder between 1863 and 1873 sprang largely from the theological misgivings of James Begg and his reactionary supporters: pietists of a rather old-fashioned kind like Andrew Bonar and Kenneth Moody Stuart, and ultra-Calvinist warriors of the so-called 'Highland Host' like John Kennedy of Dingwall.

On the other hand, the 1860s also provided many signs of a new spirit. What has been described as a 'religious upheaval' took place among Church of Scotland elders who were finding enforced subscription of the confessional formula increasingly hard to bear: their revolt proved abortive, but showed that Scotland shared the discontent which led England to accept the laxer terms of the Clerical Subscription Act in 1865. Old-style Sabbatarian views took something of a beating at the hands of Norman Macleod in the Auld Kirk and Walter C. Smith in the Free. Taylor Innes, the Edinburgh advocate, produced not only his famous volume on *The Law of Creeds in Scotland* but also an exceedingly thought-provoking essay, 'The Theory of the Church and its Creed', which had some percipient things to say about the various types of confession to be found in history and about the limited effectiveness of any confessional statement whatsoever. And a Free Church Moderator (William Wilson, 1866) came surprisingly near Macleod Campbell's position after the trial in 1831 when he declared: 'We claim no infallibility for [the Confession], or for ourselves who declare our belief in the propositions which it contains. It is the Word of God which only abideth forever. ... It is open to the Church at any time to say, We have obtained clearer light over one or other or all of the propositions contained in this Confession, we must review it; the time has come for us to frame a new bond of union with each other, a new testimony to the world. If this freedom do not belong to us, then indeed we are in bondage to our Confession, and renounce the liberty wherewith Christ has made us free.'

The 1870s were equally eventful. There was another flurry of

B

heresy trials: Fergus Ferguson, David Macrae, Robert Wallace, William Knight — not to mention the heresiarch Robertson Smith. And all the while the new, more liberal views were being widely disseminated, not now by ministers in obscure places (like Rosneath) or remote ones (like London) but by men of eminence and weight like Tulloch, Macleod, T. M. Lindsay and Alexander Whyte. Scotland — as A. M. Fairbairn, viewing the scene from Oxford, remarked in the *Contemporary Review* of December, 1872 — was drifting further and further away from the theology of the Westminster Divines. But of course vast changes were by this time well under way in the wider world beyond Scotland; and in the development of Scottish religious thought there is increasing evidence of continental and English influences. Both Cairns the United Presbyterian, and Tulloch the Auld Kirker were much at home in Germany, and they were followed by a steady stream of theological students until the Kaiser's War diverted them from Leipzig, Berlin and Tübingen to the Marne, Gallipoli and the Somme. The impact of English thinking was possibly even greater, mediated as it was through countless books, periodicals and newspapers; and in the England of Victoria doubt and infidelity and intellectual unsettlement were making steady inroads upon the old certainties.

Among the more striking — and pervasive — manifestations of the new climate of thought were the following: a fresh, and probably quite unprecedented, sense of history ('None of them', Tulloch remarked of the great Confessions, 'can be understood aright simply by themselves, or as isolated dogmatic utterances, but only in connection with their time and the genius and character of the men who framed them'); a fresh picture of the natural world (Robert Flint, professor of Divinity at Edinburgh from 1876 until well into the next century, once declared his 'willingness to review the confessional doctrines of Creation, origin of man, and Fall, in the light of the assured results of science and history'); a fresh estimate of human nature (Principal Rainy told the Free Church Assembly in 1891 that seventeenth-century thought had been marked by 'a sparingness and timidity' in recognising those 'elements in human nature which reminded them of its original greatness'); a fresh moral sensitivity (Professor Charteris, an administrative innovator but a theological conservative, could confess on one occasion that he had 'always held the expression of Calvinism in our Confession of Faith to be ruthless and hard'); a fresh tentativeness (as Rainy put it in 1880, current theology tended to ask, 'Did not all those theologies overdo the confidence of their interpretations and the sweep of their conclusions?'); a fresh tolerance ('The Church of Scotland', said Flint in 1881, 'has no right to tolerate sceptical teaching and fundamental heresy, but neither has she a right to repress variety of opinion, or to act in any inquisitorial spirit, or to violate constitutional procedure, or to treat all errors as heresies, or to be over-rigid with any man'); a fresh preference for the apologetic rather than the dogmatic spirit (Tulloch told his students as early as 1864 that 'men no longer heed utterances which are not weighty in argument as well as in tone, nor bow before a condemnation which is not reasoned as well as authoritative'); a fresh awareness — probably because of imperial expansion and missionary enterprise — of the need for a truly comprehensive Gospel (Professor A. R. MacEwen described the Westminster system as 'an exclusive one, concerning itself mainly with the position and the prospects of believers, and furnishing only a few loopholes from which furtive glances can be taken at the justice of God's providence and the breadth of His mercy in dealing with all His children'); and a fresh approach to evangelism (Carnegie Simpson wrote concerning Moody's first campaign in 1874 that 'The preaching of a "free Gospel" to all sinners did more to relieve Scotland of the old hyper-Calvinist doctrine of election, and of what the theologians call limited atonement ... than did even the teaching of Macleod Campbell').

Against this background of criticism and reassessment, the various Churches took up the task of redefining their relationship to the Confession; and from approximately 1860 on to 1910 (or even 1921) there raged what might be called The Great Confessional Controversy. The United Presbyterians led the way — perhaps because of a long-standing tradition among them of relatively liberal biblical interpretation, perhaps because their exceptional zeal for overseas missions had confronted them more insistently than others with the problems posed by the unevangelised heathen, perhaps because at least one chapter of the Confession (that on 'the magistrate') had long been modified among them on account of its allegedly persecuting and intolerant implications. Things came to a head in the late seventies, by which time two alternatives seemed to offer themselves to the Synod. On the one hand, use of the Confession as a theological test might be given up altogether and perhaps a new statement devised; on the other hand, the old Standard might be adhered to, while at the same time redefining the Church's attitude to it and allowing ministers and office-bearers some freedom in their interpretation of it. Under the guidance of John Cairns, its revered College Principal, the Synod opted for the second alternative.

The special committee set up to deal with the problem reported in 1878, recommending that candidates for the ministry or the eldership should in future signify their acceptance of the Confession in the light of a newly-drafted *Declaratory Statement* which took account of (or maybe simply reflected?) some of the changes in attitude just examined. The four opening paragraphs of this declaration dealt with certain peculiarly controversial topics in the original Confession: 'the doctrine of redemption', 'the doctrine of the divine decrees', 'the doctrine of man's total depravity', and the doctrines concerning the ultimate destiny of the heathen and of children who die in infancy. Each of these paragraphs had the clear purpose of guarding against certain extreme or erroneous inferences that had sometimes been drawn from the high Calvinism of Westminster; and, in particular, of balancing (whether permissibly or not is another question) the limitation of effectual grace to the elect with the proclamation of the love of God for all mankind. Two less significant paragraphs followed; but the Statement closed with the celebrated 'conscience clause' whose value to troubled souls can hardly be exaggerated. 'In accordance with the practice hitherto observed in this Church' — so ran the memorable phrases — 'liberty of opinion is allowed on such points in the Standards, not entering into the substance of the faith, as the interpretation of the "six days" in the Mosaic account of the Creation: the Church guarding against the abuse of this liberty to the injury of its unity and peace.'

The committee's recommendations were duly adopted by the Synod, Cairns assuring them that he did not regard the Statement as either contradicting or cancelling Westminster doctrine but simply as 'checking and counterbalancing it, giving a counterpoise to what otherwise might be looked upon as too strong and extreme'. So from 1879 onwards the Declaratory Act was part of the law of the United Presbyterian Church, and a milestone in Scottish history had been quickly and unspectacularly passed. In 1892 the Free Church followed suit in a similarly-worded Declaratory Act, and in 1910 the Church of Scotland produced (after obtaining parliamentary permission to do so) an altered formula of subscription which required no more than acceptance of the Confession as the Church's Confession together with profession of belief in 'the fundamental doctrines of the Christian faith contained therein'. None of the major Presbyterian Churches in Scotland was any longer bound in every particular by the utterances of Westminster. The old exclusiveness (and also the old definiteness and consistency) of Reformed theology was at an end, and the confessional revolution had reached its goal.

No advance has been made during the last seventy years or so upon the devisings of Cairns and Rainy and their contemporaries — manifestly imperfect though these were. (Two questions which spring to mind are: firstly, do they reconcile the irreconcilable? and secondly, what are 'the fundamental doctrines' and 'the substance of the faith' to which reference is so confidently made?) The 'Articles Declaratory of the Constitution of the Church of Scotland in Matters Spiritual', 1921 and 1926, still speak of the Westminster Confession as 'the principal subordinate standard of the Church of Scotland ... containing the sum and substance of the faith of the Reformed Church', though claiming for the Church the right to modify it or even to frame a new doctrinal statement. And under the formula of 1929 ministers still profess to believe 'the fundamental doctrines of the Christian faith contained in the Confession of Faith of this Church'.

Whether or not the Church of the 1980s and 1990s will remain content with this situation must be left to others to answer. But the historian cannot refrain from hoping that, whatever the men of the future may make of their doctrinal inheritance, they will not fall short of their Victorian predecessors in the exercise of those twin virtues whose separation has always boded ill for the Scottish people but whose conjunction, in religion as in many other areas of life, has invariably been for their good: respect for the past together with refusal to be enslaved by it.

THE TEACHING OF THE CONFESSION

Revd Dr Sinclair B. Ferguson

The purpose of this chapter is to *describe* the theology of the Confession of Faith rather than to *assess* its relative strengths and weaknesses. In the following chapter such an assessment will be made. But if we are to be able intelligently to assess the Confession for ourselves it is of primary importance that we have some familiarity with its contents and the sources of its teaching.

The contents of the Confession can be readily summarised. It consists of thirty-three chapters of unequal length, expounding what its authors would have thought of as the system of doctrine contained in Holy Scripture. The chapters can be grouped conveniently as follows:

Chapters I–V	*God, his Word, Being and Works*
Chapters VI–XVIII	*Man, his sin and restoration through Christ*
Chapters XIX–XXIV	*God's Law, Man's liberties and duties*
Chapters XXV–XXXI	*The Church, its fellowship and ordinances*
Chapters XXXII–XXXIII	*The Last Things.*

To the basic exposition proof-texts are added. It is not generally realised that these were not part of the Westminster Assembly's original work, but were added by the Assembly from October 1646 by order of the English Parliament.

This five-fold division (or any other division we cared to make) cannot adequately convey the thrust of the Confession's teaching. What kind of theology does it contain? The most concise answer is that the composers gave expression to a theology which is *Calvinistic* in emphasis, *Federal* in its basic structure, and *Evangelical* in its view of the relationship between God and man. These characteristics will become clearer by examining in turn both the content of the doctrine of the Confession, and the historical character of its theology.

The Teaching of the Confession

The theology of the Reformed Churches since the sixteenth century has always been linked with the name of John Calvin (1509–64). In his magnificent compendium of theology, *The Institute of the Christian Religion*, he brought together the great emphases of the gospel which had been rediscovered during the Reformation. There is no doubt that the theology expressed in the Westminster Confession is dependent upon his teaching. In many places (although not all) its teaching reflects his powerful influence.

1. *God, his Word, Being and Works*

When the Westminster Assembly met, one of the critical issues with which it was faced was: What is the source of authority for Christian faith? Is it Reason, or the Church, or some 'Inner Light'? If anything this problem has become increasingly important since the seventeenth century. In chapter I the Confession gives a detailed and unequivocal answer. Authority is vested in Scripture. But this in itself raises a number of subsidiary questions which the Confession proceeds to answer. Why is Scripture necessary? (I.i) What books does it contain? (I.ii, iii) Why is it authoritative? (I.iv) The exposition thereafter explains how we come to believe that Scripture is the Word of God: by the inner persuasion and testimony of the Spirit (I.vi). The contents of Scripture are both sufficient and clear enough to bring men to God (I.vi, vii). The principle by which we are to understand its message is by comparing Scripture with Scripture (I.ix).

The purpose of Scripture is practical rather than theoretical. It preserves and propagates truth so that men may come to the knowledge of God (cf. I.i). Why then begin with the Bible? Of course other, earlier Confessions had done so (The First Helvetic Confession, 1536; The Formula of Concord, 1576; The Irish Articles of Religion 1615, on which the Westminster Confession is partly based). But the reason for the order is more theological than historical. The God of the Christian, revealed in Christ, can now be known through Scripture. There is no other God and no other gospel than Scripture reveals.

This introduction brings the Confession to the most important theological question of all. *Who is God?* Our answer to this determines all our thinking. The conflict between Jesus and the Pharisees, for example, can be traced back to their opposing answers to it. Is God a legalistic God, or a God of grace?

God is 'immutable, immense, eternal, incomprehensible ...' (II.i). The Confession draws attention to the *attributes* of God. It would be a mistake to think that it therefore wanted to emphasise the static rather than the dynamic aspects of his character (just as it would be a mistake to argue that the Shorter Catechism's question, What is God? suggests its writers viewed God as a thing rather than a person, a 'What' rather than a 'Who'). For one thing, God is 'most loving, gracious, merciful, long-suffering, abundant in goodness and truth, forgiving iniquity, transgression and sin' (II.i). Furthermore there is a special emphasis in the Confession on the Fatherhood of God in a separate chapter devoted to the Christian's adoption into God's family (XII). Nevertheless what the Westminster divines ransack language to express is the character of God *in himself.* They emphasise his independence and self-sufficiency, his freedom and sovereignty. The position is expressed in these words:

> God hath all life, glory, goodness, blessedness, in and of himself; and is alone in and unto himself all-sufficient, not standing in need of any of his creatures which he hath made, not deriving any glory from them, but only manifesting his own glory, in, by, unto, and upon them: he is the alone fountain of all being, of whom, through whom, and to whom, are all things; and hath most sovereign dominion over them, to do by them, for them, or upon them, whatsoever himself pleaseth.
>
> (II.ii)

The Confession is endeavouring to express as fully as possible the truth that God really is God.

The full implications of this are worked out later in the controversial third chapter when the Confession expounds 'God's Eternal Decree'. In a manner characteristic of Reformed theology (and imitating the concerns of the apostle Paul in Romans 9), this chapter sets out to express the *freedom, righteousness* and *mystery* of God's dealings with men. According to the Confession, God, in his free mercy, in vindication of his righteousness and justice, and in sovereign mystery, chooses some for salvation and is 'pleased ... to pass by, and to ordain [others] to dishonour and wrath for their sin' (III.vii). At this point the Confession is clearly dependent upon the tradition of Augustine and Calvin. It would be naive to imagine that the Assembly found this an easy chapter to frame. On at least twenty different days they discussed its contents. Their concern was to emphasise that man has no claim upon the grace of God and no right to salvation. If any man receives salvation it is entirely because of the free love of God. More than this, space forbids us to say.

2. Man, his sin and restoration through Christ

According to the Confession, God's dealings with men are invariably covenantal. In this way he expresses his 'condescension' (VII.i). Two covenants govern the history of man. Before the Fall God made 'a covenant of works wherein life was promised to Adam, and in him to his posterity, upon condition of perfect and personal obedience' (VII.ii). Under this covenant man enjoyed 'freedom and power to will and to do that which is good and well pleasing to God; but yet mutably, so that he might fall from it' (IX.ii, cf. IV.ii). But Adam did fall (VI.i, ii), and because he was the constituted representative of the whole human race, all men sinned in his sin (VI.iii; VII.ii). As a consequence men are 'bound over to the wrath of God, and curse of the law, and so made subject to death, with all miseries spiritual, temporal, and eternal' (VI.vi). To alleviate this situation God has made a second covenant, the covenant of grace 'whereby he freely offereth unto sinners life and salvation by Jesus Christ, requiring of them faith in him, that they may be saved' (VII.iii).

Two emphases in the Confession's teaching here are noteworthy. The first is that the way of salvation in both Old and New Testaments is exactly the same. The Westminster divines realised that the difference between the message of the Old

Testament and that of the New is not the difference between salvation by obedience to the Law and salvation by faith. On the contrary, both Old and New Testaments point to the one covenant of grace which 'was differently administered in the time of the law, and in the. time of the gospel'. The Old Testament contains the promise of Christ, the New contains the fulfilment of that promise. The purpose of God's Law, therefore, was not to provide salvation through works, but to point to the way of salvation through faith in Christ (cf. Rom. 4: 13 ff; Gal. 3: 15 ff.).

The second emphasis is on the work of Christ as Saviour, or 'Mediator' (VIII). Following Calvin's lead (*Institute* II.XV), the Confession teaches that Christ fulfilled the office of Prophet, Priest and King in order representatively to restore man to fellowship with God. This restoration took place, according to the Confession, through the *obedience* of Christ (VIII.v). In what is often termed his 'active obedience' he fully discharged the will of God, and in his 'passive obedience' he bore the judgment of God on man's sin (VIII.iv). It is worth noting in passing that the Confession endeavours to avoid the common distortion of Christ's work which suggests that as Saviour he wrests forgiveness from an unwilling Father. On the contrary, 'It pleased God, in his eternal purpose, to choose and ordain the Lord Jesus his only begotten Son, to be the Mediator between God and man' (VIII.i). By his death he 'hath fully satisfied the justice of the Father' (VIII.v). According to this teaching, Christ has taken man's place under the just judgment of God and accepted all the implications of his guilt. This is the doctrine of penal, substitutionary atonement.

3. *Ethics, Ecclesiology and Eschatology*

The rest of the Confession is largely devoted to the life of the Christian in its various dimensions. Chapter XIX expounds the Law of God. The Ten Commandments are seen as a republication of the original will of God for man's life. This is the key to understanding the Confession's teaching that while salvation cannot be gained through obedience to the law, the law remains as 'a rule of life' (XIX.vi) for the Christian. It also has evangelical and civil functions as well as this ethical one. It reveals men's sin and restrains them. But neither the ceremonial nor the political aspects of the Old Testament laws remain in force, since they basically involved a temporal application of the abiding principles enshrined in the moral law.

Closely related to this theme is that of Christian liberty. Here the Confession's axiom is that 'God alone is Lord of the conscience' (XX.ii). This has a very specific meaning. It means that the Christian is free to be obedient to God's Word. He is under no obligations except those sanctioned by Scripture.

The teaching given on worship and the sabbath follows the basic principle earlier enunciated that the ordinances of creation are continued in all ages of the Church, although the way in which those ordinances are applied may vary from dispensation to dispensation. Keeping the sabbath is 'a positive, moral, and perpetual commandment' (XXI.vii). The precise day which is kept may vary (ibid.). Since the ceremonial aspects of the law have been abolished (XIX.iii) it follows that the mode of worship will be different under the New Testament.

The Christian also acknowledges the authority of the State. The Confession teaches the divine ordination of government, the lawfulness for the Christian of service to the State, the possibility of a 'just' war, and the responsibility of the magistrate to ensure that the unity, purity and discipline of the Church is maintained. It is therefore in the power of the magistrate to call and attend synods. The General Assembly of the Church of Scotland in 1647 (when the Confession was examined and approved) limited this power to 'kirks not settled'. The situation envisaged by the Westminster Assembly was one in which the State did not set itself in opposition to the Church. Against any other background its words would have a strange and almost sinister ring to them.

The Confession briefly outlines the doctrines of marriage and divorce in chapter XXIV. Christians are to marry 'only in the Lord' (XXIV.iii), and not within the degrees of consanguinity forbidden in Scripture (cf. Leviticus 18). Divorce is possible, but on two grounds only — adultery, and 'such wilful desertion as can no way be remedied by the church or civil magistrate' (XXIV.vi). After divorce remarriage is permitted 'as if the offending party were dead' (XXIV.v).

Chapters XXV to XXXI summarise the doctrine of the Church. There is a tendency in the exposition to equate the Church with the Kingdom of God (XXV.ii). The Church is described in terms of its *visibility* and *invisibility*. The Confession intends by this distinction to distinguish between the profession which is seen by men and brings us into the fellowship of the Church (visible), and the reality of faith which is seen only by God and brings us into communion with the elect (invisible). The distinction is time-honoured and in some ways helpful. But even those who have strong sympathy with the Confession's exposition have raised questions about its ultimate validity. Something of this hesitation appears in the statements of the Confession itself. It affirms that the catholic Church 'is invisible' (XXV.i); that the 'visible Church' is also catholic (XXV.i); and that the catholic Church has 'been sometimes more, sometimes less visible' (XXV.iv)! Inevitably in a seventeenth-century document strong language is used in describing the Roman Catholic position. It is striking that the strong language the Scots Confession had used for Roman Catholicism in general, the Westminster Confession applied to the Pope in particular. It should of course be remembered that Roman Catholicism was seen, in seventeenth-century Scotland and England, not only as a false religion, but also as a powerful political menace. It is impossible really to understand the writing of that time without appreciating what a feared influence this was.

Three chapters (XXVII–XXIX) are devoted to the sacraments. They are seen to have four basic functions: (a) they represent Christ and his finished work. Through the actions involved in baptism and the Supper they also re-present him in order to convey visibly to the Church the truth which is presented verbally in the preaching of the Word; (b) they are confirmations of Christ's love and death 'sealing all benefits thereof unto true believers' (XXIX.i); (c) they are external marks which distinguish the Church from the world; and (d) they are outward signs of our engagement to be servants of Christ. Because the Reformed emphasis in sacramental teaching is that the sacraments exhibit grace and elicit faith, baptism is applicable both to believers and to their children. The efficacy of the sacraments is received through faith alone, but it is not 'tied to that moment of time wherein it is administered' (XXVIII.vi).

The concluding chapters deal with the Last Things and are readily summarised. The Confession affirms the reality of Christ's return, of the Last Judgment, and of Heaven and Hell. The last day, when all men and angels shall be judged has already been appointed, but remains unrevealed. On it God will finally manifest the glory of his mercy and the glory of his justice. This assurance should make the Christian watchful and create in him a spirit of expectancy, so that he is always prepared to say: 'Come, Lord Jesus, come quickly' (XXXIII.iii).

Theological and Historical Background

Like every Creed or Confession the Westminster Confession was written against a background of history and theology in which the orthodoxy of the day was being questioned. We can trace between its lines concern about the influence of Arminianism, Socinianism, Rationalism, Romanism and Mysticism. While this fact no more disqualifies the Confession from contemporary usefulness than it does the great Ecumenical Creeds, it does alert us to the presence of historical influences in its teaching.

A full discussion of these emphases is clearly beyond the scope of a short survey, but several of them may be mentioned by way of illustration.

1. We have already noted the primary place allotted to Scripture by the Confession. Neither Calvin nor Knox gave it the same primacy of position. In *The Institute* it appears in Book I: VI; in the *Scots Confession* of 1560, at chapter XIX. But by the time of the mid-seventeenth century the inspiration and authority of Scripture had become a central issue in theological debate. Scripture's authority was now questioned by various forms of Rationalism and Mysticism. Hence the opening chapter of the Confession. Of it the famous church historian Philip Schaff wrote, 'No other Protestant symbol has such a clear, judicious, concise, and exhaustive statement of this fundamental article of Protestantism' (*Creeds of Christendom*, I, 767).

Despite the passage of three hundred years, it would still be true to say that this doctrine is as great a dividing line as it was then. It is, to speak frankly, one of the chief issues which divides Presbyterians from one another, and in the Church of Scotland attitudes to Scripture are often the hidden cause of differences in ecclesiastical discussion.

2. The Westminster Confession contains no chapter on the Holy Spirit. Again this is, in part, due to the influence of Calvin's *Institute* (although Calvin himself has been well described as 'the theologian of the Holy Spirit'). It may also be due to the controlling influence of the biblical teaching in which the Spirit is seen as the *agent,* and not as the *object* of faith (cf. Jn 16: 7–15). Thus, in the Confession, the ministry of the Spirit permeates many of the doctrines. The chapters on Scripture (I.vi), God (II.iii), Election (III.vi), Creation (IV), Christ (VIII.ii, v, viii), Calling (X.i, ii, iii, iv), Justification (XI.iv), Adoption (XII), and Sanctification (XIII) all contain references to the way in which the Spirit applies Christ's saving work to the Church. Indeed, contrary to some contemporary suggestions, there was probably more interest in and concern about the work of the Spirit in the seventeenth century when the Confession was written, than at any time since. It is also a very real question whether the kind of pronouncement the Church might be expected to make today about the work (and the gifts) of the Spirit, is really suited to a document in which a confession of faith is made.

Another apparent hiatus in the Confession's teaching is the absence of a chapter on Evangelism. Undoubtedly this phenomenon is historically explicable. Evangelism had not been thought of before as a mark of the Church. Yet it is clear in the New Testament that a Church, or a Christian who does not in some sense evangelise is a contradiction in terms. It is interesting to notice that the Savoy Declaration of Faith and Order of 1658, which is a Congregationalist revision of the Westminster Confession, added a chapter entitled 'Of the Gospel, and of the Extent of the Grace thereof'. Yet even this left room for further emphasis on the duty of the Church to take the gospel to every creature in obedience to Christ (Matt. 28: 18–20).

Similarly it is the historical tradition of Creeds and Confessions which explains the absence of any exposition of the life and ministry of Christ.

3. There is room only to mention the chief theological influence on the Confession's teaching. B. B. Warfield, perhaps the most erudite proponent of the Confession during this century, wrote that 'The architectonic principle of the Westminster Confession is supplied by the schematization of the Federal theology' (*The*

Westminster Assembly and its Work, p. 56). Something must be said about the influence of this school of thought.

The word 'federal' is derived from the Latin *foedus*, a covenant or treaty. It describes the doctrinal emphasis which emerged in the Reformed Churches of Europe in the sixteenth and seventeenth centuries, when the centrality of the Bible's teaching on God's covenant grace to men was rediscovered. Undoubtedly this fresh understanding was directly due to a renewed interest in the historical study of Scripture, and also to the Reformers' usual practice of consistent, consecutive and practical exposition of Scripture in their preaching. But it was given fresh impetus by the Anabaptist accusation that the mainstream Reformers had thoughtlessly acquiesced in the 'unbiblical' practice of infant baptism. In response the Reformers argued that God had made one covenant with men with Jesus Christ at its heart, administered in two dispensations, the 'old' and the 'new'. Since the children of believers received the initiatory sacrament of this covenant in the restricted administration of the 'old covenant', they must also receive the initiatory sacrament of baptism in the 'new covenant'.

In Calvin's *Institute* this emphasis was brought to maturity, and the covenant of grace was recognised as the theological key to the Scriptures. He emphasised that all the covenants in Scripture were but the unfolding of the one great covenant of grace, experienced in the promise of Christ in the old dispensation, and his presence in the new. Christ, Calvin stated, is the substance of God's covenant with man.

Through the influence of the Scotsman Robert Rollock, English preachers like William Perkins, and Europeans like Ursinus, Gomarus and Cocceius (all famed theologians in their day), a new emphasis appeared. A twin-covenant theology began to develop. If all God's dealings with men are covenantal (so it was argued) then he must have entered into a covenant with Adam in the Garden of Eden, long before the covenant with Abraham. From the time of Rollock's two treatises, *Certain Questions and Answers respecting God's Covenant* (1596), and *Treatise on Effectual Calling* (1597), this first covenant was known as 'the covenant of works'. It is in the Westminster Confession that this teaching came to find its classical expression: God entered into 'a covenant of works, wherein life was promised to Adam, and in him to his posterity, upon condition of perfect and personal obedience' (VII.ii). When this covenant was breached by the Fall, 'the Lord was pleased to make a second, commonly called the Covenant of Grace whereby he freely offereth unto sinners life and salvation by Jesus Christ' (VII.iii).

This twin-covenant theology moulds the Confession's teaching in a variety of ways precisely because it provided the fundamental perspective of its authors. It inevitably influenced the Confession's teaching on God, on the condition of man in sin, the work of Christ as Saviour, and the pattern of spiritual experience in which men are brought from *under* the covenant of works *into* the covenant of grace. It is a salient characteristic of the Puritan teaching expressed in the Confession that men are brought to Christ by 'law–work', in which they are made conscious of their guilt, and of their bondage under the old covenant, and thus seek refuge in the new covenant in Christ — hence the acts of 'personal covenanting' in which our forefathers engaged.

Many questions are raised by this theology. Scholars have pointed out its remarkable genius for holding together in tension the great objective realities of the gospel with subjective experience of its power. It has, on the other hand, been regarded by its critics as a strait-jacket breeding doubt and fear. With respect however, an acquaintance with the personal experience of the Westminster divines rather indicates that many were men of liberty and joy; in cases like Samuel Rutherford, men of ecstasy, even if 'made of extremes' (as he once wrote). Nevertheless, the covenant of works doctrine raises many unanswered problems.

For many years, for all practical purposes in Scotland, this covenant theology has been a dead letter in class-room teaching of theology and in pulpit exposition. That is no longer the case. In recent years a recovery of the knowledge of the Covenant God has taken place, both in academic and scholarly writing, and in the preaching of God's word. In a striking way the issues which caught the imagination of the seventeenth century are capturing the minds of Christians in the twentieth century. In this context it should be remembered that the writers of the Confession did not possess, nor did they expect, agreement with every jot and tittle of its contents. It was framed, as George Gillespie (one of the Scots commissioners) suggested in debate, to provide latitude of understanding, so that 'every one may enjoy his own sense'.

Discussion of the Confession's teaching was in fact one of the writers' chief aspirations. Not for many years has such a discussion of the theology of the Confession been so vital a matter for the well-being of our Church as it is today.

STRENGTHS AND WEAKNESSES OF THE WESTMINSTER THEOLOGY

Revd Professor James B. Torrance

The Westminster Confession of Faith is a clear, lucid statement of Puritan thought at its best. It is a remarkably comprehensive statement of 'moderate Calvinism' and although it is the first post-Reformation confession to enshrine the 'federal scheme', with the distinction between a covenant of works and a covenant of grace, it is a mild statement compared with the views of John Owen, Samuel Rutherford, David Dickson or *The Sum of Saving Knowledge*.

There were broadly speaking four types of divine at the Westminster Assembly:

1. Moderate episcopalians (e.g. Dr Ussher — though he may never have attended)
2. Independents (e.g. Thomas Goodwin)
3. Erastians (e.g. Dr John Lightfoot)
4. Presbyterians (e.g. Matthew Newcomen)

acting with the assistance of the Scottish Commissioners, among whom were Alexander Henderson, Samuel Rutherford, George Gillespie, and Robert Baillie. Considering the variety of views and Church backgrounds represented, it is a remarkably uniform systematic statement of the theology of the 'second Reformation'. Doubtless the variety of the standpoints represented led to the mild statement of Calvinism which it embodies.

I

The Practical Character of the Documents

The major strength and weakness of the Westminster Documents lie in their practical character, due to the practical remit of Parliament and due to the Puritan concern to apply the doctrines of grace to the faith and life of the believer.

1. The Westminster Assembly was appointed by the Long Parliament to give advice on the reformation of the Church in England, against tyranny, popery and Arminianism. It had the practical concern therefore to reduce tyrannical power and meet the need for an ordering of Church government based on the teaching of the Bible.

The *Parliamentary Ordinance* of 12 June 1643 declared the purpose to be 'the calling of an Assembly of learned and godly Divines, and others, to be consulted with by the Parliament for the setting up of the *government* and *liturgy* of the Church of England; and for vindicating and clearing the *doctrine* of the said Church from false aspersions and interpretations'. Its concern was to take away the prelatic hierarchy of the Church which was condemned as 'evil, offensive, and burdensome to the kingdom' and find a form of government, liturgy and discipline, as well as a statement of doctrine, agreeable to the Word of God. Should the relationship between the civil and ecclesiastical governments be Erastian, Melvillian (the two kingdom theory) or Separatist? Some commissioners, like Lightfoot and Coleman, were both Presbyterian and Erastian. The Assembly finally agreed to a modified Erastian view that there should be a national Church, and most agreed it should be Presbyterian.

There was throughout a practical concern for unity and uniformity:

(*a*) There was the ecclesiastical concern to bring the Church of England into closer agreement with the Church of Scotland. The Scottish Church had been already calling for this agreement and uniformity.

The Assembly began with the concern to revise the Thirty-nine

Articles of the Church of England, but two things happened to change the direction of the Assembly. Firstly, there was the urgent practical need to produce rapidly a pattern of Church government in the context of the Puritan Revolution and the reaction to Laud and the claims of the divine right of kings. There was also the immediate shortage of ministers, as so many were acting as chaplains in the Civil War. Secondly, the change of fortunes on the field of battle meant that the Long Parliament sought help from the Scots. This led to the signing of the Solemn League and Covenant between English Puritans and Scottish Covenanters. Here we see the blending of a double practical concern — a civil and a religious. Robert Baillie wrote: 'The English were for a civil league and we for a religious covenant.' The English concern was for the Constitution; the Scots had a more specifically religious concern for purity of doctrine and worship, in reaction to Laud and to carry forward the concern of the National Covenant. It is significant that it was Parliament which instructed the Assembly at Westminster to stop revising the Thirty-nine Articles, and to deal first with the issue of Church government. This was in order to make ordinations possible again, for none had taken place since the abolition of episcopacy. When the divines resumed their doctrinal work some months later, they adopted an entirely new approach to produce a new Confession.

(b)   There was also the concern for *peace*. The title of the missive taken to the Westminster Assembly by the Scottish Commissioners was 'Our Desires concerning Unity in Religion and Uniformity of Church Government as a special means to conserve Peace in his Majesty's Dominions'. It then stated that 'It is to be wished that there were one Confession of Faith, one form of Catechism, one Directory of all the parts of the public worship of God ... in all the parts of his majesty's dominions'. It was the concern of the Solemn League and Covenant to seek a covenanted uniformity of doctrine, worship and government. The remit to the Assembly was to advise Parliament as to how this could be done.

(c)   *Politically*, the practical concern was to oppose all forms of tyranny and to seek a 'most firm and stable union between the two kingdoms of England and Scotland' — hence the 'civil league'.

(*d*) *Theologically* the aim was 'the utter extirpation of popery, prelacy, heresy, schism, superstition and idolatry — and for the settling of the so much desired union of this whole island in one form of Church government, one Confession of Faith, one common Catechism, and one Directory for the Worship of God' (*Acts of the General Assembly of the Church of Scotland, 1643*).

The result was:

(1) *The Form of Presbyterial Church Government*, so creative of later Presbyterianism.

(2) *The Directory for the Publick Worship of God*, 1645. This was not primarily a theological document, but emerged out of the concern for freedom in worship and 'free prayer', motivated by opposition to set forms of liturgy, as in the Book of Common Prayer, and a desire for 'the covenanted uniformity in religion betwixt the churches of Christ in the kingdoms of Scotland, England and Ireland'.

(3) *The Confession of Faith*, 1646. Its chapters were at first called 'Articles of Religion'. The English Parliament declined to give it the title of a 'Confession of Faith', but received it as 'The *Humble Advice* of the Assembly of Divines', because it did not begin with the words 'I believe' or 'we believe' and because it was produced out of the remit to guide Parliament as to the form of religion in terms of which it was to promote reformation and covenanted uniformity. So Parliament felt free to omit ch. XXX of Church Censures, ch. XXXI of Synods and Councils, and also portions of other chapters on Marriage and Divorce, the Civil Magistrate, etc.

This practical remit was evident to the Scottish Commissioners, one of whom declared, 'This is no proper Assembly, but a meeting called by Parliament to advise them in what things they were asked' (Baillie's *Letters*). This is of great importance in evaluating the documents as a Confession of a Church, which it was to become officially in Scotland, but not in England. It was not produced in the first instance as a Church Confession. This may account for much of the emphasis, as well as for certain striking omissions.

(4) The *Larger and Shorter Catechisms* show the practical concern to instruct the young and advance the cause of reformation and Christian nurture.

2. The practical character of the Confession is also seen in the powerful Puritan concern to *apply the doctrines of grace to life.* Behind the document we see Puritan biblical preaching, and the concern for authentic religious experience, and, through it all, the Puritan doctrine of the Sovereignty of God and the Puritan understanding of the scheme of salvation. The Bible is the major premiss, with the conviction that all life should be based on biblical precedent and biblical principles. It is significant that when the work was finished, the House of Commons made an order that Scripture proofs should be added. In all these many ways it was to exercise an enormously formative influence on the religion of Scotland and on Presbyterianism throughout the English-speaking world.

It is significant that the largest part of the Confession is given over to the question as to HOW the benefits of the Covenant of Grace are applied to believers (IX–XVIII), followed by chapters on Law and Liberty (XIX–XX), worship and the sabbath day (XXI) and Civil matters (XXIII–XXIV). Only then does the Confession turn to the doctrine of Church and sacraments (XXV–XXXI), leaving the 'last things' to the last chapters (XXXII–XXXIII).

Many of these chapters on the Christian life are magnificently stated but their weakness lies not so much in what they say as in what they do *not* say. For example, this is apparent in the chapter on Sanctification (XIII), summarised in the Shorter Catechism Q.35.

> Sanctification is the work of God's free grace, whereby we are renewed in the whole man after the image of God, and are enabled more and more to die to sin and live unto righteousness.

It is well stated, but the concern is entirely with sanctification *in us*, i.e. sanctification subjectively considered, with not a word about Christ as the One who assumed our humanity and sanctified it *for us* by His life in the Spirit (John 17:19; Heb. 2:11; 10:14; I Cor. 1:30), nor about our participation in Christ. The practical concern is paramount with its interest in the application of the benefits of Christ, that believers be 'more and more quickened and strengthened in all spiritual graces, to the practice of true holiness'. But this practical concern means that the emphasis moves away from what God has done *for us and for mankind in Christ* to what *we* are to do to know that we are among the elect and in covenant with Christ.

Likewise in the statement on baptism (XXVII and Shorter Catechism Q.94) the sacrament 'doth signify and seal *our* ingrafting into Christ, *our* partaking of the benefits of the Covenant of Grace, and *our* engagement to be the Lord's'. The emphasis is on what has to happen to us and in us, rather than on the One Baptism of Christ, in which we are given to participate, as Calvin expounds it in the *Institute* (IV.15.6).

II

Weaknesses in the Confession

Again these emerge, not so much in what it says in individual articles, but in the whole *schema* and understanding of the *ordo salutis* vividly illustrated by Perkins' diagram from *The Golden Chain* (1590), at the end of this chapter. The pattern is no longer the Trinitarian one of the Creeds or Calvin's *Institutio* of 1559, but is dominated by the eternal Decrees and the scheme of Federal Theology. This in turn produces serious weaknesses in the understanding of God, of grace, and of the Holy Spirit.

1. *The place given to the Doctrine of the eternal Decrees*
When we consider the following Confessions:

1553   *Forty-two Articles of* Cranmer
1562   *Thirty-nine Articles*
1595   *Lambeth Articles* of Whitgift
1615   *Irish Articles* of Ussher
1643–48   *Westminster Confession*
(and the 1658   *Savoy Declaration*)

we see two things,

(a) the growing emphasis on election and the doctrine of the decrees of God — on double predestination, and

(b) the decided move to a view where *election precedes grace,* so that the interpretation of the Person and Work of Christ is subordinated to the doctrine of the decrees, and seen as God's way of executing the decrees for the elect. The result is that grace is limited to the redemption of the elect.

Thus the doctrine of the decrees of God in the tradition of Theodore Beza and William Perkins becomes the major premiss of the whole scheme of creation and redemption. This is clearly a move away from the Scots Confession, where election is placed after the Article on the Mediator, in the context of Christology. It is also a move away from Calvin who expounds election at the end of Book Three of the *Institute* as a corollary to grace, after he has expounded all he has to say about the work of Father, Son and Holy Spirit, and after his exposition of Incarnation and Atonement.

When the doctrine of the decrees becomes the major premiss, what happens? Here again we see the influence of the pragmatic Western legal mind with its preoccupation with the How? question and its genius for putting decisions into effect — of applying principles, be they the 'principles' of biblical teaching in the life of the Church, or the application of law in concrete situations (cf. the lengthy exposition and application of the law in the Larger Catechism, savouring of casuistry), or the decrees of God. The basic questions therefore become:

(1) How does God execute the eternal decrees? By Creation, Providence, permitting the fall, Redemption, effectual calling, etc.

(2) How does God secure the Redemption of the elect?

(3) How does God effectively apply the benefits of the Covenant of Grace to the elect, in the life of the believer and in the gift of the means of grace, Church, Word and sacraments?

(4) How does the believer know if he is among the elect and someone for whom Christ died, and how can he find assurance of salvation?

(5) Under what conditions is marriage (or divorce) lawful, or can magistrates lawfully exercise power?

What is the result of this pragmatic approach?

(*a*) This is probably what gives rise to the feeling of 'Legalism' in the documents.

(*b*) There is a danger of subordinating theology to the category of means and ends, of being more interested in asking How? than Who?

(*c*) It leads to the subordination of grace to election.

(*d*) It leads logically to the Bezan and post-Reformation doctrine of a 'limited atonement' and particular redemption. The 1720 'black Act' of the General Assembly condemning *The Marrow of Modern Divinity* cited the Westminster Confession, VIII.viii, as teaching limited atonement. Limited atonement was certainly regarded as the 'orthodoxy' of the Westminster documents, as we see in the condemnation of McLeod Campbell in 1831. But it was not so taught by John Calvin. The subject was the occasion of much controversy in Scotland.

(*e*) The doctrine of the double decree and the corollary of a limited atonement affected the practice of celebrating the Lord's Supper. The older Scottish divines of the sixteenth century regarded the sacrament of the Lord's Supper, like preaching, as an evangelical 'converting ordinance', where Christ was held out in bread and wine to be received by all in faith. But the seventeenth-century federal Calvinists like George Gillespie (one of the Assembly commissioners) rejected this view on the grounds that only the elect may come to the sacrament — and that means in practice that only those who show 'evidences' of election are 'worthy' to come! The sacrament is not a converting ordinance but a 'badge of our conversion'. So there comes into Scotland the dangerous 'Romish' view that the sacrament is a seal of our repentance! It was this which tragically started that kind of fencing of the tables which has in effect kept multitudes of people from communicating. It also led to the introspective tradition of self-examination for evidences of election, with the resulting loss of joy and assurance.[1]

2. *Federal Theology*

The Westminster Confession enshrines the 'federal scheme', and is the first post-Reformation confession to do so. It is beyond the scope of this paper to elaborate. But the issue is one of enormous importance, because federal theology, which first developed among the Puritans of England, came into Scotland about 1596 under Robert Rollock, and soon became the absolute criterion of orthodoxy and was equated with 'Calvinism'. The basic concept is that of *foedus* ('covenant' or 'contract').

(a) Fundamentally it teaches that God made a Covenant of Works with Adam, and in him with all men, making eternal life conditional on keeping its terms — the Covenant of Law, the *foedus naturae, foedus operum.* Hence all men are related to God as contracting Sovereign, law giver and judge. But only the elect are related to God by grace, for God has made a second covenant for them in Christ, the Covenant of Grace — the *foedus gratiae.* The Marrowmen were to protest that this second Covenant of Grace was also presented in conditional terms, making God's grace to the elect conditional on their faith and repentance and personal holiness. The doctrine of a Covenant of Works (whose conditions Christ fulfils for the elect) implies that God is a contract-God, and denies that God is related to all men in Love (Agape). John Owen and Jonathan Edwards took this to its logical conclusion that Justice is the essential attribute by which God is related to all as Judge, but the Love of God is arbitrary! But what doctrine of God is that? It is a concept of God derived from 'reason', 'the light of nature' and Western notions of 'natural law' and 'the law of contract' and read back into the Bible. But it is not the biblical view that God is Love (Father, Son and Holy Spirit) in his innermost Being and that his Being is manifested in all his activities, in Creation, Providence, as well as Redemption.

(b) The federal scheme, as expounded by the great Puritans like William Perkins (the most widely read writer at the beginning of

1. See McInnes, *The Evangelical Movement in the Highlands of Scotland*, A.U.P., 1951, on the influence of Thomas Hog of Kiltearn on the fencing of the tables; also R. T. Kendall, *Calvin and English Calvinism to 1649*, O.U.P., 1979.

the seventeenth century, whose powerful influence is seen in the Westminster divines) taught that the two covenants of Works and Grace (Law and Grace) are the two stages by which God executes the eternal decrees and brings the elect to salvation.[2]

(c) The federal scheme is built thus on the *priority of Law over Grace.* Calvin, in the 1536 edition of his *Institute,* followed the pattern of Law–Grace in Luther's *Short Catechism,* but subsequently abandoned it as not true to the Bible. Law is the gift of grace, spells out the obligations of grace and leads to grace — its fulfilment in Christ. That is the inner meaning of *Torah.* That is true not only in the life of Israel, *but in Creation.* So Calvin never taught any 'covenant of works' nor would have. But the English Puritan tradition, in its practical concern to use the law as a schoolmaster to bring men to Christ, universalised from that use of the law ('law–work'), read it back into Creation and into the doctrine of God, and grounded the Two Covenants on it. But this is to go back to the Mediaeval *ordo salutis* (of Alexander of Hales, etc.) of Man–Law–Sin–Repentance–Grace. This was precisely the order which Calvin struggled to reverse! No Puritan theologian embodied the Western *ordo salutis* more thoroughly than John Owen in his doctrine of the Christian life. So much Scottish preaching has embodied this same *ordo* — and given rise to that 'legal strain' in preaching against which Thomas Boston and the Marrowmen protested, and which led McLeod Campbell to argue — as Calvin had done — that 'the filial is prior to the judicial'.

(d) The federal theologians in this way adopted a Western *Nature–Grace Model,*[3] interpreting Nature in terms of the orders of creation (the *foedus naturae*), but only the Church and the elect in terms of the order of redemption (the *foedus gratiae*). God creates Adam the child of nature, who can discern the Law of Nature by the light of Reason, as the 'federal' head of the race. But out of the mass of fallen mankind, he elects some for salvation and in grace sends Christ to be the redeemer of the elect and Head of His Church. The sphere of nature and the sphere of grace are certainly both interpreted in terms of the overarching Sovereignty of God. But, on this model, Christ is the Mediator,

2. See Perkins, *The Golden Chain.*
3. See the appended diagram.

not for all men, but only for the elect, and consequently only the Church is interpreted Christologically ('The Form of Presbyterial Church Government'). The State, the civil order, is thus interpreted non-Christologically in terms of natural law and the light of reason (in terms of 'common grace' by later Calvinists). But this dualistic model fails to take adequate account of the New Testament doctrine of the Headship of Christ over all creation and all nations as Mediator. The Nature–Grace model is the inevitable corollary of following Beza and Perkins in making the doctrine of the double decree the major premiss, because thereby grace and redemption are restricted to the Church — the *numerus electorum* — and the life of the believer. Hence we can see why the Confession has so much to say about the *believer* (his effectual calling, justification, sanctification, etc.) but so little about the world at large and nothing about race relations. But has the confessing Church no evangelical word about the Headship of Christ to proclaim to the State and the political arena as in the Barmen Confession of 1934? The doctrine of the double decree is thus not just one article among others. It has become determinative of the whole Puritan federal scheme.

3. *Strengths and weaknesses in the Doctrine of God*

On the one hand, the Westminster documents lay a powerful stress on the Sovereignty and Freedom of God in all areas of life. 'The earth is the Lord's and the fullness thereof.' This is stated with great dignity and sobriety. It is clearly Augustinian, refusing to ground God's decrees on any foreknowledge of human good works, yet stressing human responsibility for sin. There is a profound sense, as in Calvin, of the Majesty of God. The term 'sovereignty' among the Puritans and Scots, however, is acquiring political overtones — that the Sovereignty of God is above the 'sovereignty' of king and people (cf. Rutherford's *Lex Rex*).

On the other hand its weakness is that it seems to stress the Will of God as sovereign and free (the divine *arbitrium* of Rutherford) rather than the Being of God as a God of Love whose freedom is always the freedom of his love. What God is in his Being (Father, Son and Holy Spirit) he is in all his acts, and what he is in his acts, he is eternally and antecedently in his Being — Holy Love. Hyper-Calvinism can lead to a new Sabellianism by implying that God is loving *toward* some men but not essentially *in his Being*. Is this not why it has bred such a lack of assurance in Calvinistic Scotland, where devout minds have been tortured by the question — 'Am I one of the elect? Does God love me? Am I worthy enough to go to the sacrament? How can I know if I am one of the elect?'

C. G. McCrie in his *The Confessions of the Church of Scotland* (pp. 59 ff.) comments on the very frequent occurrence in the Confession of the phrase '*It pleased God* ... according to the *counsel of His own will*' in its exposition of the decrees, of creation, of providence, the covenants, revelation, redemption, effectual calling, etc. He gives copious illustration of this and sees it as the most distinctive feature of the Confession in its stress on the Sovereignty of God. 'The light of nature sheweth that there is a God, who hath lordship and sovereignty over all' (ch. XXI — of Religious Worship and the Sabbath-day). The Ten Commandments in the federal scheme are the republication of the Law of Nature. Hence the sabbath was regarded as part of the Law of Nature and the contract of Nature, to be enshrined in civil law. Hence Parliament could pass laws about sabbath keeping. But we might ask, is this the Old Testament being interpreted in the light of its fulfilment in Christ, or is it being interpreted in the light of some natural theology — 'the light of nature'? Calvin was always careful to argue that just as circumcision and the blood sacrifices of the Old Testament were fulfilled in Christ and replaced by baptism and the Lord's Supper, so the Jewish sabbath found its fulfilment in Christ who is our peace, and is replaced by the Christian day of the Lord, the Easter anticipation or 'sacrament' of the rest of the Kingdom of God. The Old Testament is thus interpreted evangelically, and not as providing a set of legal precedents. When creation is alternatively interpreted 'in the light of nature' it leads too readily to the arbitrary God or the contract God according to one's interpretation of 'nature' and 'natural law'. It obscures the clear teaching of the Bible that the God who is Father, Son and Holy Spirit in his innermost Being created all men for sonship, love and communion. But we only have that understanding of creation when creation is seen in the light of its fulfilment in Christ 'by whom and for whom all things were created'. The federal scheme has abandoned the Irenaean doctrine of recapitulation of all things in Christ, for a Western Nature–Grace model.

4. *Strengths and weaknesses in the Doctrine of Grace*

Most certainly the intention of the Westminster divines was to expound the doctrines of grace. But we are bound to ask a number of questions, to some of which we have already referred.

(*a*) The Confession gives priority to law over grace by embracing the federal scheme. This can lead us as in the Western *ordo salutis*, to interpret grace too readily as the God-given answer to human need, i.e. too anthropologically. So it is in the Latin West that the phrase 'the means of grace' occurs as though God provides the means we need to find the solution to our human problems. But this can obscure the fact that grace is God giving himself to us in love in Christ, and doing for us in Christ what we cannot do for ourselves. Grace means Jesus Christ clothed with his Gospel.

(*b*) Consequently there is a tendency to separate grace from Christ in the Latin Western tradition as 'something' we need, e.g. sacramental grace, 'graces' as equivalent to blessings, etc. No doubt these 'graces' or benefits are purchased for us by Christ. But the pragmatic concern is to ask, HOW do we receive these blessings, under what conditions can they be appropriated, administered, applied, etc? This is not only true in the Roman tradition, but persists in the Protestant Calvinist tradition as well. For example, the often quoted phrase, 'Grace is sufficient for all but efficient only for the elect' implies that grace is quantitatively construed in causal terms, and derives from mediaeval notions of merit.

(*c*) This separation of grace from Christ can be reinforced by the Augustinian language of sacraments as 'visible signs of invisible grace'. This is not only suggestive of Platonic dualism, but implies an understanding of grace as something you 'get' in the sacraments. But that implies that the meaning of the sacraments is being interpreted in ways which treat them as 'rites' of the Church, rather than in terms of Christ giving us himself and the gift of participating in what he has done and is doing.

5.   *Weaknesses in the Doctrine of the Holy Spirit*[4]

Where the dominant interest is in applying to believers the benefits of the Covenant of Grace, the tendency can be to think of the Holy Spirit in terms of efficient causality as the agent in effectual calling and applying the blessings of the Gospel — and so in ways which can be too impersonal. The Spirit is not just the 'instrumental cause'. Again the weakness in the Confession is not so much in what it says, but in what it does *not* say about the Holy Spirit. There is a wealth of biblical teaching here which is absent, about the Holy Spirit as the bond of union between the Father and the Son, in whose communion we are given to participate through the Spirit of adoption; that Jesus is the recipient of the Spirit in our humanity in sharing a common anointing; that He is the Mediator of the Spirit and the Dispenser of the Spirit; that there is an indissoluble bond between Christ and the Spirit (expressed in the *filioque* — which the Confession acknowledges) in virtue of which we are given to participate in the life of Christ — in His intercessions and His mission to the world. The doctrine of the Spirit would doubtless have been given a fuller place had the Westminster divines adopted a Trinitarian pattern for the Confession.

4. In 1903, the Presbyterian Church in the U.S.A. added two chapters, ch. 34 'On the Holy Spirit' and ch. 35 'On the Love of God and Mission' — doubtless to modify the severity of the doctrine of the decrees.

*The Nature–Grace Model of
Federal Theology (Puritan Calvinism)
as reflected in the Westminster Confession*

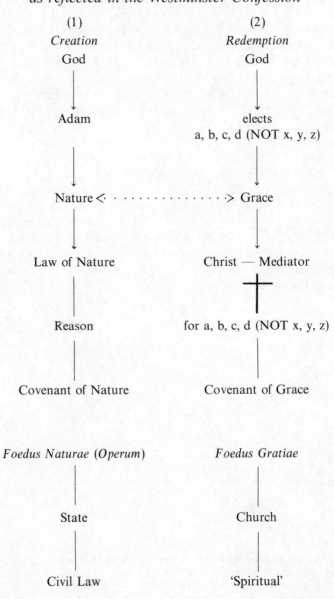

(1)	(2)
Creation	*Redemption*
God	God
Adam	elects
	a, b, c, d (NOT x, y, z)
Nature <· · · · · · · · · · · · · ·> Grace	
Law of Nature	Christ — Mediator
Reason	for a, b, c, d (NOT x, y, z)
Covenant of Nature	Covenant of Grace
Foedus Naturae (Operum)	*Foedus Gratiae*
State	Church
Civil Law	'Spiritual'

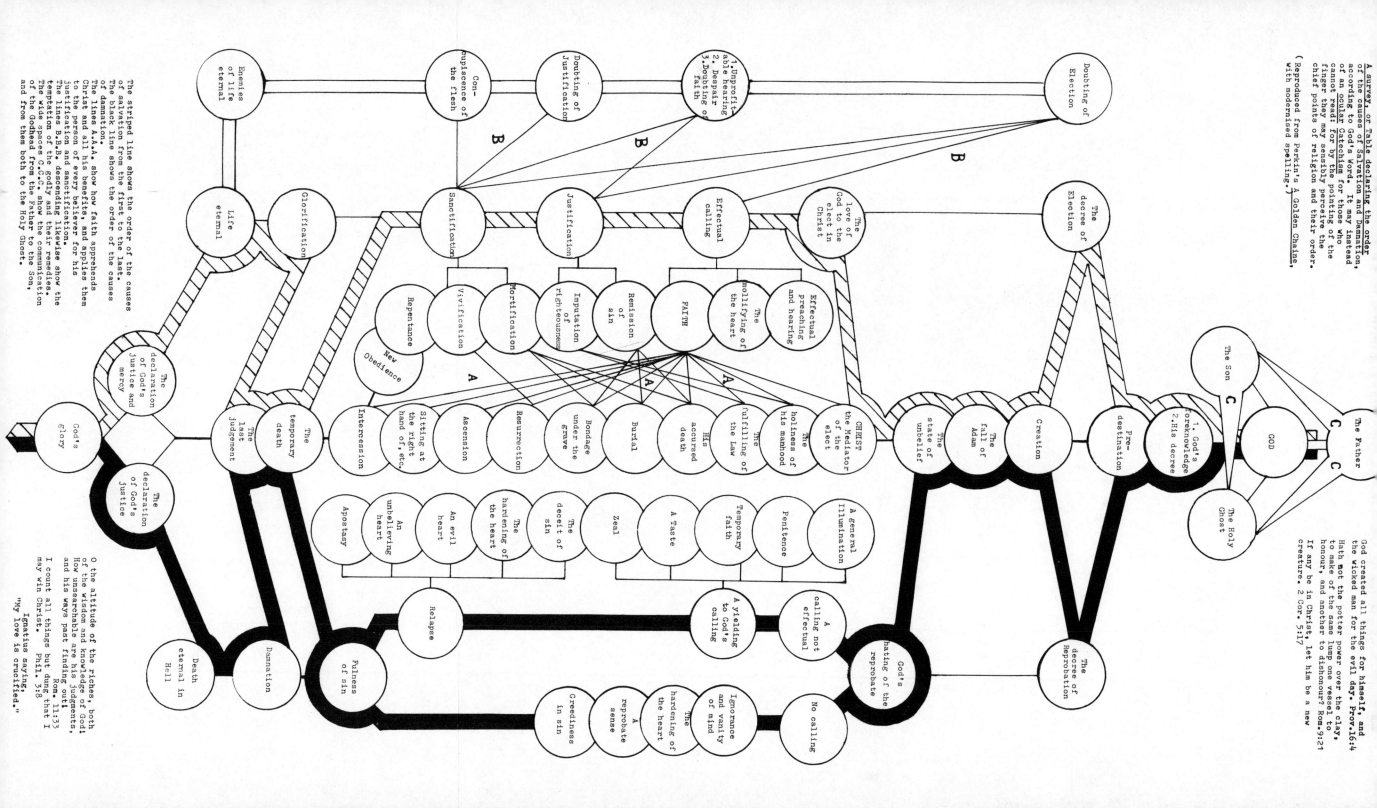

A survey, or Table declaring the order of the causes of Salvation and Damnation, according to God's Word. It may instead of an ocular Catechism for those who cannot read: for by the pointing of the finger they may sensibly perceive the chief points of religion and their order.

(Reproduced from Perkin's A Golden Chaine, with modernised spelling.)

God created all things for himself, and the wicked man for the evil day. Prov.16:4 Hath not the potter power over the clay, to make of the same lump one vessel to honour, and another to dishonour? Rom.9:21 If any be in Christ, let him be a new creature. 2 Cor. 5:17

1. God's foreknowledge
2. His decree

The striped line shows the order of the causes of salvation from the first to the last. The black line shows the order of the causes of damnation. The lines A.A.A. show how faith apprehends Christ and all his benefits, and applies them to the person of every believer for his justification and sanctification. The lines B.B.B. descending likewise show the temptation of the godly and their remedies. The wide spaces C.C.C. show the communication of the Godhead from the Father to the Son, and from them both to the Holy Ghost.

O the altitude of the riches, both of the wisdom and knowledge of God! How unsearchable are his judgements, and his ways past finding out! Rom. 11:33 I count all things but dung that I may win Christ. Phil. 3:8

Ignatius saying, "My love is crucified."

THE WESTMINSTER CONFESSION:
THE LEGAL POSITION

Professor Francis Lyall

There are many elements in the legal position of the Westminster Confession, and not all of them are self-consistent. I am not required here to make a judgement on these matters as a court would have to do, or to give a legal opinion on a question put to me. Hence I do not seek to impose order where I find disorder. What I do seek to do is to indicate possible areas of difficulty, where matters could be decided if brought to the courts of law, the civil institutions whose business it is to decide such matters. I am not arguing a case. The points indicated below could all be trenchantly argued were it to come to that, but the purpose of this chapter is to inform.

First, however, I would say clearly that in my view the current position of the Confession is one of creative uncertainty. At present the various wings of opinion within the Church of Scotland are talking to each other. That rapprochement would terminate abruptly were the quasi-geological fault lines between the theological groupings within the Church to be put under undue stress, particularly by the introduction of legal process, but also by an untimely effort to impose solutions. What I hope to show here are the areas of risk buried within the façade of the law which might be involved. But first, it may help to narrate the legal materials in their historical order.

I

The materials which we have to consider are the statutes concerning the Church of Scotland and its Confession, the religious provisions of the arrangements for the Union between the kingdom of Scotland and the kingdom of England, some later legislation, notably the Church of Scotland Act 1921, which declared lawful the Declaratory Articles which were eventually approved by the General Assembly in 1926,[1] and (though this is more nebulous) the practice of the Church. There is also some judicial discussion of these matters. Finally there is the Basis of Union, on which the Church of Scotland and most of the United Free Church united in 1929.[2]

That there should be a close association between Church and state was usual in former centuries. It was the deliberate policy for a variety of reasons that one Church should be given statutory recognition, which might amount to a statutory basis for its very existence. The Reformation statutes of 1560, re-enacted for technical reasons in 1567, show an amalgam of purposes, the safeguarding of the new and the displacement of the old. The Scots Confession was ratified and approved by Parliament as 'The Confession of Faith and Doctrine Believed and Professed by the Protestants of Scotland ...'. Later, other steps were taken to purify, defend and aliment the Church by civil statute. Similarly the General Assembly Act 1592 c.8 established the Presbyterian government of the Church through civil statute. That was the usual practice.

It is not surprising therefore, that Parliament approved the Westminster Confession in 1649, two years after the Assembly had approved it. Following the problems of the next forty years, the Confession was carefully secured on the occasion of the new monarchs, by the Confession of Faith Ratification Act 1690 c.7, and its position along with other essential church matters, including Presbyterian government, was secured by Scottish and English statutes as part of the Union of 1707.

Historically, the next important step was the Disruption of the Church in 1843 over the question of patronage and the right of the Church to govern itself. In 1900 a major part of the Free Church sought to join with the United Presbyterian Church. The

---

1. In terms of its s.4, the 1921 Act was then brought into force on 28 June 1926 by the Church of Scotland Order in Council (S.R. and O. 1926) No. 841. Lawyers tend to talk of the 1921 Act, ecclesiastics of the 1926 Articles.
2. See my *Of Presbyters and Kings*, Aberdeen University Press, 1980, for an extended discussion.

resultant court case showed that such a step could raise questions of law especially in regard to matters of property. Therefore, when the United Free Church (the eventual product of the union of most of the Free and the U.P. Church) began discussions with the Church of Scotland, an attempt was made to avoid future difficulty by getting Parliament to pass the 1921 Church of Scotland Act, declaring lawful the Articles Declaratory of the Constitution of the Church of Scotland in Matters Spiritual. These Articles were then approved by the Church in 1926, and are an integral part of the Basis of Union of 1929.[3]

Such then, in short outline, are the major legal materials in their historical context. We can now turn to discuss them.

II

In 1981, churches in Scotland are given considerable freedom in law, and are protected in their property, activities and rights. The rules of contract are used to give them a sphere of jurisdiction over their members, a sphere into which the civil courts will not intrude, provided that there is no question of wilful impropriety. The property of churches or denominations is held under the laws of trust for each church or denomination. But the state does require that the identity of a church or denomination shall be clear to it before the church will be recognised and protected in its activities and property. The church must have a known identity.

The identity of a church or denomination is a complex matter, involving what is known in law as its 'original principles'. These are the fundamental principles, to which the organism claiming to be a church adheres. These principles will obviously involve beliefs, and may also involve the system of government and authority in the church. Within the identity of the church, there is freedom so long as the original principles of the church are adhered to. If the majority of the members, or of the governing bodies of the church, do not so adhere, those within the church who continue to hold to the original principles will be able to

3. The Basis of Union, which is binding in a way which the Plan of Union is not, is printed in J. T. Cox, *Practice and Procedure in the Church of Scotland*, 6th ed. by D. F. M. MacDonald, 1976, 386–95. (Hereafter cited as 'Cox'.)

resist change, and the majority will have to yield their legal rights and interest in the church to the minority. The matter may be solved by agreement,[4] but the rights of the minority will be enforceable through the civil courts as happened in the Free Church case.[5] The civil courts have indicated that it is possible in law for a church to hold as one of its original principles the ability or power wholly to change its fundamental principles, by, for example, having as its only fundamental principle, adherence to its governing body. However, I know of no such church recognised by the state, and such is not the position of the Church of Scotland as I understand it. The identity of the Church of Scotland is limited, and is bounded. The freedom of the Church of Scotland is therefore a freedom within its identity. It is not a freedom to change its identity.

Subject to what will be said under III, the Church of Scotland Act 1921, declaring lawful the Articles Declaratory of the Constitution in Matters Spiritual, was an important step in the granting of freedom to the Church and it is important in the current definition of its identity. As noted above, the Articles scheduled to the Act were adopted by the General Assembly of 1926, and form an integral part of the Basis of the 1929 Union.

The First of the Declaratory Articles is a short and summary statement of the identity of the Church. The bulk of it is a statement of the faith in almost credal form. As Cox states, the Church claims freedom to follow the Spirit, interpreting the Scriptures to successive generations,[6] but there are limits. In Article I we also read that the Church of Scotland 'adheres to the Scottish Reformation'. That imposes a limit on the identity of the Church.

4. When the majority of the United Free Church united with the Church of Scotland in 1929 the U.F. Church assets were divided by agreement between those entering union and the U.F. Church continuing.

5. *General Assembly of the Free Church of Scotland: Bannatyne* v. *Lord Overtoun*, (1904) 7 F.(H.L.) 1; [1904] A.C. 515. These are references to Fraser's Reports of cases in the House of Lords, and to the official English Appeal Cases series. Argument before the Lords, and their decision was printed in R. L. Orr, ed., *The Free Church of Scotland Appeals*, 1903–4, 1905. See also op cit. n.2, 105–110. In fact Parliament passed the 1905 Churches (Scotland) Act under which Commissioners divided the property between the parties, on an equitable basis. Except where there were many buildings or other circumstances, property was allocated to the Free Church where it retained one-third of the former membership.

6. Cox, 2–3.

Further specification is given with the first mention of the Confession, which comes in Article II: 'The principal subordinate standard of the Church of Scotland is the Westminster Confession of Faith approved by the General Assembly of 1647, containing the sum and substance of the Faith of the Reformed Church.' This means that the Westminster Confession is very closely built into the identity of the Church, even though reference to it is not incorporated in Article I. I believe it was not so incorporated as being a human document, subject to error: Article I states theological and historical truth.

In any event, notwithstanding what will later be said regarding the removal or replacement of the Confession from the Articles, the position of the Confession is not wholly dependent upon those Articles for its legal significance and application. As noted, Article II states that the Confession contains 'the sum and substance of the Faith of the Reformed Church'. That form of words was not newly minted by the Articles, but closely echoes the formulation of the Confession of Faith Ratification Act 1690 c.7, an Act passed on the insistence and with the approval of the Church to secure its position once more. Further, while the precise language is not found in it, the Act of the 1647 General Assembly on the Confession of Faith, with its explanations, clearly also approves the Westminster Confession, finding it upon due examination 'to be most agreeable to the word of God, and in nothing contrary to the received doctrine, worship, discipline, and government' of the Kirk.[7] It would be difficult to recede from that position, even on the argument that the Westminster Assembly was eighty years after the Reformation. When one considers the Scots Confession of 1560, and compares it with its successor, the Westminster Confession gives significant evidence of the doctrinal and other positions (including church government) of the Scottish Reformation to which the Church adheres.

But how closely is the Westminster Confession built into the identity of the Church as a matter of law rather than of evidence? Several points emerge here, which might produce conflict. Either the Confession is irremovable, or its position can be modified by

---

7. Act of Assembly, August 27, 1647, Session 23: printed in *The Subordinate Standards and other Authoritative Documents of the Free Church of Scotland*, 1955, xxvii–xxviii, and in some editions of the Westminster Confession.

unanimous agreement, or its position can be modified subject to other procedures involving less than total agreement. Then, if it is removable, must its position be filled by another confessional statement?

III

There are on the statute books Acts of a basic constitutional nature giving the Confession legal status both within the Church and within the state. It is not absolutely clear that the 1921 Act consigns those Acts to oblivion. Certainly s.1 of the Act provides that:

> The Declaratory Articles are lawful articles, and ... no limitation of the liberty, rights and powers in matters spiritual therein set forth shall be derived from any statute or law affecting the Church of Scotland in matters spiritual at present in force, it being hereby declared that in all questions of construction the Declaratory Articles shall prevail, and that all such statutes shall be construed in conformity therewith and in subordination thereto, and all such statutes and laws in so far as they are inconsistent with the Declaratory Articles are hereby repealed and declared to be of no effect.

But it is, of course, the art and corruption of the legal mind to see complexities. These words may not give the Church a total freedom to do as it will with the Confession. The references to adherence to the Scottish Reformation in Article I, and to the Confession as 'containing the sum and substance of the Faith of the Reformed Church' according to Article II, themselves raise doubts. The entrenchment of the religious provisions of the Treaty of Union and relative Acts also comes into play. These provisions may be fundamental and unalterable provisions of the British constitution, from which the Articles and the Act cannot derogate.

Some might argue that the position of the Confession is so entrenched in the ordinary constitutional law of the state that it is irremovable, without a revision of the arrangements for the Union of Scotland and England. The argument runs that the Confession and the Presbyterian government of the Church were secured by the Confession of Faith Ratification Act 1690 c.7. They were further protected by being excluded from the Union negotiations by the Act 1705 c.50, and by their incorporation in an Act of Security, the Protestant Religion and Presbyterian Church Act 1707 (1706 c.6).[8] In the actual Union, the position of the Church was therefore secured, and the 1706 Act was inserted, as had been required, in both the Union with England Act 1707 c.7, and its English equivalent, the Union with Scotland Act 1706 (6 Anne c.11). The religious provisions of the Union were stated to be among the fundamental and essential provisions of the Union, only some of which were alterable by the Union Parliament.

This raises two questions, first the fact that some of such 'unalterable' provisions have been subsequently repealed, and second, and more generally, the doctrine of the sovereignty of Parliament.

As to the first, it may be observed that where there has been repeal of a provision stated to be fundamental and essential to the Union, such repeal has occurred with the consent of interested parties. For example the Church did not oppose the abolition of the requirement that a Professor sign the Confession on induction to his chair.[9] Where there has been opposition Parliament has not proceeded with the matter.[10]

The question of the sovereignty of Parliament then arises. On the orthodox English view our current Parliament is sovereign and unfettered in its powers, taking on the attributes of the English Parliament which it replaces. Indeed it is rare to find an Englishman who considers the Union Parliament as being other than its English predecessor enlarged by the addition of some Scots representation. It has, however, been indicated in Scottish

8. Apart from other formal provision in the Act, it also requires the sovereign to take an oath on accession to preserve inviolable the Protestant religion as then established. The Accession Declaration Act 1910 contains the current formula.
9. See op. cit. n.2, 121–3 for the steps taken. Subscription was made 'no longer necessary' by s.5 of the Universities (Scotland) Act 1932, having been in abeyance for 'lay' chairs since 1853.
10. Thus D. N. MacCormick, [1972] Public Law, 174–9 quotes Hansard, 1872 H.L. Deb. vol. 210, col. 1990 and 1873 H.L. Deb. vol. 214, col. 1738, that the Union agreements were the reason why the Scottish courts (protected by the Union) were not reorganised along with the English courts by the Supreme Court of Judicature Act 1873.

cases and juristic writing that the Union Parliament may have limitations built into its constitution by virtue of the Treaty of Union and relevant legislation.[11] On this view it is arguable either that the 1921 Act itself is contrary to the Union, or that its language must be interpreted so as not to contravene the terms of the Union. If this is so either the position of the Westminster Confession, entrenched by the Union is not alterable, or, more reasonably, it is not alterable unless by the consent of the whole Church. Parliament, limited by the Union agreements, would not have had the power to enact otherwise.

This may seem arcane, but it is on precisely such kinds of arguments that many of our major constitutional developments down the years have founded.

We now turn to the content of the 1921 Act and the Articles.

IV

I tend to prefer the proposition that, within the compass of the 1921 Act's approval of the Articles, the position of the Confession can be adjusted. The Church claims fidelity to the Word of God and the leading of the Spirit. Councils may err. These two

---

11. See op. cit. n.2 pp. 78–83. *Minister of Prestonkirk* v. *Wemyss* (1808) Morison's Dictionary of Decisions, App. 'Stipend' No. 6 (Connell on *Tithes* (1815) vol. 3, pp. 310 ff.); *McCormick* v. *Lord Advocate* 1953 Session Cases 396 (esp. Opinion of Lord Cooper at 411); *Gibson* v. *Lord Advocate* 1975 Scots Law Times 134. J. D. B. Mitchell, *Constitutional Law*, 2nd ed., 71–2, n. 34: T. B. Smith, *Basic Rights and their Enforcement*, 1979, app. 'Note on the Union Agreement of 1707'; *The United Kingdom: Scotland*, 1955, pp. 641–50; 'Two Scots Cases' [1953] 69 Law Quarterly Review 512; 'The Union of 1707 as Fundamental Law' [1957] 2 Public Law 99: K. W. B. Middleton, 'Sovereignty in Theory and Practice', (1952) 64 Juridical Review 135; 'New Thoughts on the Union between England and Scotland', (1954) 66 Juridical Review 37: G. Marshall, 'Parliamentary Supremacy and the Language of Constitutional Limitation', (1955) 67 Juridical Review 62 (cf. 'What is Parliament? The Changing Concept of Parliamentary Sovereignty', (1954) 2 Pol. Stud. 193): D. N. MacCormick, Review of S. A. De Smith, *Constitutional Law*, [1972] Public Law 174–9; 'Does the United Kingdom have a Constitution? Reflections on *MacCormick* v. *Lord Advocate*', (1978) 29 Northern Ireland Law Quart. 1–20.

 For an English case indicating the contrary, see *British Railways Board* v. *Pickin* [1974] A.C. 765. It was alleged that a Private Act had been improperly obtained, but the courts were stated to have no powers to examine the proceedings of Parliament. This is not quite the question of the powers of Parliament.

propositions could conflict, but the fact remains that the Confession is a statement of the faith expressing an understanding of that faith drawn from the Bible. Were all church members to agree, it would be better that that agreement should be given legal effect than that the property and assets of the Church should pass to the state as a result of the failure of the trust purposes for which they were held, owing to departure from the Confession.

However, universal agreement is very unlikely, and we must therefore consider the mechanisms for change. What, then, are the powers of change within the terms of the 1921 Act?

In terms of Article VIII, alteration of the Declaratory Articles is permitted using a modified Barrier Act procedure. This requires reference to Presbyteries in at least two immediate successive years. Two-thirds of Presbyteries must approve the proposal for the Assembly to enact it, but, as in 1974, the Assembly is not bound to enact a duly approved proposal. Amendments to the overture, though not major revision, may be suggested by Presbyteries on the first reference, or the Assembly may amend the proposal itself. A substantial alteration of the proposal means that the procedure has to start again. If less than two-thirds of Presbyteries do not approve an overture in its final form, the same or a similar proposal may not be sent down to Presbyteries until five years after such failure has been reported to the General Assembly.

What is the extent of the power to amend the Articles by Article VIII procedure? First, the power given is to alter or modify the Articles. Whether this includes the power to eliminate a reference to the Confession of Faith is open to argument. In 1969 the Opinion of the Procurator on the then proposals of the Panel on Doctrine was that, given s.1 of the 1921 Act quoted above, reference to the Confession could be deleted.[12] I am not quite so sure, and the fact that a different opinion was obtained on a later version of the proposals shows that there may be an arguable point here.[13] Section 3 of the 1921 Act preserves the

---

12. *Reports to the General Assembly of the Church of Scotland*, 1970, Report of the Panel on Doctrine, 171 at 180–2; op. cit. n. 2, 160–2.
13. *Westminster Confession of Faith, Report of the Panel on Doctrine 1971. Some comments and criticisms.* The National Church Association, October 3, 1971, 3–4; 1976 Juridical Review, 69: op. cit. n.2, 163–4.

position of the Courts in civil matters and it would be for the court to consider whether it had jurisdiction. The position of the Confession clearly could raise civil questions. Only one case has heretofore construed the ambit of the 1921 Act. *Ballantyne v. Presbytery of Wigtown* 1938 S.C. 625, concerned the appointment of a minister, not the acute matters which the Confession could raise. The majority opinion gave a wide interpretation to the Act going far beyond what was required to decide the case but the decision was not unanimous, and there are elements in the opinions of some judges which could be usefully developed.

The question that is raised by the elimination of the Confession under Article VIII procedure is, as before, the identity of the Church. Unless there is a specification of the doctrinal position of the Church, in some form of confessional statement, can it be said that the Church 'adheres to the Scottish Reformation'? The statements of Article I are too wide on their own to show that identity.

It appears that the framers of the Articles saw this point, but from the other end. Article VIII provides that any modification or addition to the Articles must be consistent with Article I, 'adherence to which, ... is essential to [the] continuity and corporate life' of the Church. Article VIII also gives the Church both power to interpret the Articles and power to determine whether any amendment of them is consistent with Article I as interpreted by the Church.

But suppose that the Church does not consider a proposal to amend the Articles to be inconsistent with Article I. Is that not an end of the matter, and does that not mean that the Church can do as it likes? After all Article IV contains strong statements. The Church has:

the right and power subject to no civil authority to legislate, and to adjudicate finally, in all matters of doctrine, worship, government, and discipline in the Church. ... Recognition by civil authority of the separate and independent government and jurisdiction of the Church, in whatever manner such recognition be expressed, does not in any way ... give to the civil authority any right of interference with the proceedings or judgements of the Church within the sphere of its spiritual government and jurisdiction.

Article V then says:

> This Church has the inherent right, free from interference by civil authority, but under the safeguards for deliberate action and legislation provided by the Church itself to frame or adopt its subordinate standards, to declare the sense in which it understands its Confession of Faith, to modify the forms of expression therein, or to formulate other doctrinal statements, and to define the relation thereto of its office-bearers and members, but always in agreement with the Word of God and the fundamental doctrines of the Christian Faith contained in the said Confession, of which agreement the Church shall be sole judge, and with due regard to liberty of opinion in points which do not enter into the substance of the Faith.

Is the Church not final, despite the language just quoted? Is its power to interpret congruence with Article I unchallengeable?

Here resides a main point of difficulty, which was raised during the passing of the 1921 Act, correctly answered by the Solicitor General in the Commons, and promptly fudged, lest the fact that the civil courts could still be involved should torpedo the bill. The compromise, which is enshrined in the 1921 Act, like most compromises, is not wholly self-consistent, and it was rendered acceptable only by certain points not being too closely scrutinised.

Solicitor General Murray, asked whether the phrase 'as interpreted by the Church' modifying the reference to Article I in Article VIII in effect meant that the Church could do as it liked, said:

> My legal opinion has been asked whether that [phrase] means that the Church as a Free Church has a power of interpretation. In law, if my opinion was asked, I think there must be a limit. It must at least be 'interpretation', and in the long run, of course, you have to have recourse to judicial interpretation. Provided that the Church loyally and *bona fide* interprets its standard as there set forth, it has the right to determine that standard. That right is only limited by the right of the judiciary, where there has been mis-interpretation or absence of interpretation, to control.[14]

14. (1921) 143 H.C. Deb. 1461. See also op. cit. n.2, 76–7.

It is clear from this, and from other remarks in the passage of the bill through Parliament, that the civil courts cannot interfere to stop the Church deciding in a particular way. But there are circumstances where the civil courts could impose property consequences.

There are two points here, first the question of consistency with Article I, and second the statement of the Church's power in Article V 'to frame and adopt its subordinate standards, to declare the sense in which it understands its Confession of Faith, to modify the forms of expression therein, or to formulate other doctrinal standards, ... but always in agreement with the Word of God, and the fundamental doctrines of the Christian Faith contained in the said Confession, of which agreement the Church shall be the sole judge.'

The power of the Church to interpret must be genuinely exercised. As the main legal architect of the Articles wrote during the negotiations:

> No institution within the State can exempt itself from the authority of the State, and no Act of Parliament can divest the State of its ultimate authority; but, under the scheme contemplated ..., any appeal to civil authority would be to the authority of the general law and not to the authority of the State as limiting in any way the action of the Church in virtue of a special relation of this Church to the State.[15]

Under the normal general principles of Scots law, in particular of public law as these have been developed, some challenge might still be brought to a Church decision. In law finality given by statute is the finality of a properly working body. The Church's freedom and finality — its being the 'sole judge' — lies within its identity. It could not, for example, adopt a unitarian stance, say that in its view that was consistent with the Trinitarian statement of Article I, and then stand on its being 'the sole judge' of such matters. The question is, short of such an extreme, when would the courts consider themselves not excluded from looking to property consequences on the lines of the Free Church case?

15. C. N. Johnston (Lord Sands), 'Church Union in Scotland', (1920) 233 Quarterly Review, 205–25 at 215.

If the Church then was clearly departing from its identity, which includes adherence to the Scottish Reformation according to Article I, and perhaps still according to the 1707 Union and all its statements, it forfeits its protection. It would not properly be exercising its powers of interpretation and legislation. That would be so even if a numerical majority in Assembly and Presbyteries claimed the contrary in the avowed exercise of the Church's power of interpretation. It therefore remains possible that were it patent that the Church was abusing its powers of interpretation and sheltering behind a plea of finality, the civil courts could take the jurisdiction reserved to them by s.3 of the 1921 Act, and apply property consequences to a Church action. For the courts that would mean awarding the property to a remnant of the Church still genuinely adhering to the identity of the Church. In the Free Church instance the civil authority stepped in to divide the property under the Churches (Scotland) Act 1905. If the matter were not so clear, it would still remain for the civil courts to consider the matter of their jurisdiction were the matter to be properly brought before them. Such a situation would, of course, be extreme, but it is not, in legal terms, inconceivable.

V

It would be much easier to demonstrate continued adherence to the Scottish Reformation were the position of the Westminster Confession as principal subordinate standard to remain, particularly because that Confession is stated by Article II to contain the 'sum and substance of the faith of the Reformed Church'. The Church has the power to 'declare the sense in which it understands its Confession of Faith' and 'to modify the forms of expression therein', under Article V. The Declaratory Acts of the United Presbyterian Church 1879, and of the Free Church 1892 and 1894 are included in the Basis of Union of 1929 as leading documents on doctrine.[16] Provided that there is congruence with the Scottish Reformation as before, further Declaratory Acts could be passed by the Church to clarify and explain particular

16. Cox, 435–47. The Basis also refers to other uniting Acts of the predecessors of the uniting churches which have also a bearing on the interpretation of the Confession. These are set out, Cox, 437–43.

matters, as was done in these precedents from our predecessors. Indeed perhaps the discussion of the 1970s paid insufficient heed to the existing Declaratory Acts as setting some sort of boundary to doctrinal variation, though it must also be agreed that they are in part incompatible and that years of failure to enforce them, through uncertainty, contribute to our present problems.

It would also be competent to raise another Confession or other Confessions to the status of a subordinate standard, without necessarily prejudicing the position of the Westminster Confession unless the newcomer were totally incompatible with the principal standard.

The remaining avenue is to replace the Westminster Confession of Faith by another which would also lie within the requirement of adherence to the Scottish Reformation. This would seem to be legally competent, assuming that the Confession can be removed. Whether it is practicable at what the Panel called in 1969 'this period of ... theological ferment'[17] is moot.

VI

So far I have been considering the general position of the Confession, and in effect looking at its function as an identifier of the Church in the eyes of external bodies. It is time to consider the Confession's position internally in the Church itself.

The position of the Confession within the Church is that in relation to ministers and elders it is a standard of faith. It is not laid on ordinary members. For them simple profession of faith suffices. For an office-bearer more must be required to preserve the integrity of the Church by spelling out more clearly of what the essentials of the faith affirmed consist. At ordination therefore both ministers and elders subscribe a formula laid down by the Church of Scotland.[18] The Preamble of this formula includes the statement that the Church holds as its subordinate standard the Westminster Confession of Faith, and the subscriber must, *inter alia*, state that he believes the fundamental doctrines of the Christian faith contained in it. It is therefore quite extraordinary

17. *Reports to the General Assembly of the Church of Scotland* 1969, 210.
18. Cox, 568–9, 573–4; the Formula for licensing which contains the same provision is at 571–2.

how many listen to the Preamble and then subscribe that formula without having read the Confession. It is quite improper for such later to discover that they do not like what is in the Confession, even with the various Declaratory Acts, and to seek to displace it. They should resign. Any other course is sheer dishonesty, which cannot make for the health of the Church.

In fact the formula of subscription is much milder than it used to be. By civil statute subscription was required by ministers in 1693, though the exact wording was a matter for the Church. The Church required subscription by elders in 1694, and tightened the formula in 1711. However, when the position was examined in 1889–1901, it was considered that the 1693 Act still might be vital.[19] Accordingly in 1905, during the enactment of the bill dealing with the Free Church case opportunity was taken to give the Church of Scotland powers regarding the formula. Section 5 of the Churches (Scotland) Act 1905 states that the formula of subscription to the Confession of Faith for ministers should be such as would be prescribed by the General Assembly, following Barrier Act procedure. The Act XIII, 1910[20] made use of that power and its provisions were revised by the uniting Church in 1929–32, as above.

But there is a problem with the present formula. While subscribers do affirm belief in the fundamental doctrines of the Christian faith contained in the Confession, the custom of the Church indicates that the Confession contains more than these fundamental doctrines. The Preamble for Ordination and Declaratory Article V refer to liberty of opinion on such points of doctrine as do not enter into the substance of the Faith, and it seems now tradition that the conscience clause does modify the Confession. However, we have no list either of all the fundamental doctrines, or even of some of them. In recent years only infant baptism has been the subject of Assembly decision (1976), and a series of decisions on marginal cases could establish a minimum content for the fundamentals of the faith. But Assembly decision on actual cases is not a desirable way of proceeding. A Declaratory Act, perhaps enumerating the doctrines affirmed by

19. A. T. Innes, *The Law of Creeds*, 2nd ed. 1904, 138–9; R. Vary Campbell, 'Spiritual Independence Constitutionally Considered', [1900] 12 Juridical Review 194.
20. Cox, 434.

the 1974 Draft Preamble as being *of* the substance of the faith, would be better. That would not close the category of fundamental doctrines, but would indicate a minimum content adhered to by the Church. An alternative might be to raise the Scots Confession to subordinate standard status. Then, by use of the existing Declaratory Acts specified in the Basis and Plan of Union 1929, and a comparison of the Scots and Westminster Confessions, some clearer notion of which doctrines the Church holds as fundamental could be arrived at by correspondence between the Confessions. We might arrive at the lowest acceptable common theological denominator within the tradition of the Scottish Reformation, to which we are bound by the First of the Declaratory Articles. The impact of the Declaratory Acts in such a proceeding would not be negligible.

Such a proceeding would not necessarily involve any alteration in the Declaratory Articles of 1926. The Westminster Confession would remain as principal subordinate standard, and the Scots Confession would be added to the other subordinate standards in doctrine, which are part of the Uniting Act 1929 (II.2),[21] but which are not mentioned in the Articles. It would, however, be possible to alter the Articles to include the enumeration of the other subordinate standards under the amending procedures provided for by Article VIII. There would appear to be no argument about that.

VII

I end where I began. The legal position of the Confession is unclear, and I reckon that many of the possible solutions to the problems which are presently encountered would open up conflicts and discussions of the law, which are better avoided. As an academic lawyer I would like to see some fully argued judicial opinions on the 1707 Union arrangements, and perhaps on the rôle of fundamental law in Scottish Constitutional Law. But that would not be helpful. The risks and damage which would ensue would be enormous. It would be an end of the current processes by which various wings of the Church are meeting, discussing and

21. Cox, 388–9.

getting to understand each other, for recourse to Law usually means an end of friendship and often respect. It may be that the time is not ripe to settle these matters, and arrive at an accommodation. If so, it certainly is not the time to force things on, and risk the intervention of legal debate. At present there is a creative uncertainty. Creation takes time.

THE RECENT DEBATE IN THE CHURCH OF SCOTLAND

Revd Roderick Pettigrew

The doctrinal position of the Church is presently defined by the first of the 'Articles Declaratory of the Constitution of the Church of Scotland in Matters Spiritual', which is generally held to describe in theological terms the identity of the post-Union (i.e. post-1929) Church of Scotland, and by the Preamble which is read at the ordination and induction of ministers and at the ordination and admission of elders. The Church of Scotland acknowledges Scripture to be its 'supreme rule of faith and life' and holds the Westminster Confession of Faith as its 'principal subordinate standard', recognising 'liberty of opinion on such points of doctrine as are not of the substance of the faith'. This last clause, commonly called the 'conscience clause', is held by many to be essential as allowing a reasonable breadth of interpretation, especially as many within the Church feel that they cannot agree without reservation to every part of the Westminster Confession.

The Church's understanding of the Confession is further modified by the Declaratory Acts of the United Presbyterian Synod, 1879, and of the Free Church, 1892 and 1894. These Declaratory Acts were adopted in the Basis and Plan of Union, 1929, among others, as 'leading documents setting forth the constitution, standards, rules and methods of the united Church'.

However, towards the end of the 1960s there was considerable concern within the Church about the teaching of certain doctrines which were allegedly heretical. It was felt that the reasonable limits of interpretation had been exceeded when some persons

72

claimed the protection of the conscience clause in apparently denying certain doctrines which others felt, equally conscientiously, to be of the substance of the faith. The Courts of the Church had difficulty in dealing with these allegations effectively, largely because the Church had not defined what was 'of the substance of the faith'.

This concern was shown when representations were made from the Presbyteries of Aberdeen and Glasgow to the General Assembly of 1968. An overture from the Presbytery of Glasgow led to the formation of a Special Committee anent the Doctrine of the Church and commissioners from the Presbytery of Aberdeen moved that 'the General Assembly instruct the Panel on Doctrine to give consideration to the place of the Westminster Confession of Faith as the subordinate standard of the Church's faith and to the references to it in the Preamble and Questions used at Ordinations with a view to offering guidance to the Church'. The first of these remits was to lead to the Panel's later preparation of the statement of belief for popular use; the second to its attempt to amend the Preamble and the Articles Declaratory.

Amendment of the Preamble and the Articles Declaratory

The Panel reported to the General Assembly of 1969 with its proposals to amend the Preamble. Guided by the wording of its remit, it proposed that the Church should depart from the concept of 'subordinate standards' and that the Westminster Confession of Faith should no longer be the 'principal subordinate standard'. Instead, the Confession was to be associated with the ancient creeds and the Scots Confession as historic statements of faith and a revised Preamble was to be prepared into which was to be inserted a short statement of fundamental doctrines, which ministers and elders would be required to subscribe on signing the Formula.

The Panel was concerned that at the all-important moment of the ordination of its ministers the Church should be able to act without reservation. Its doctrinal basis, referring to the Scriptures as its 'supreme rule of faith and life' and to the Westminster Confession as 'its subordinate standard', modified both by the conscience clause, covering items of belief which were not of the (undefined) 'substance of the faith', and by the Declaratory Acts, was felt to be complicated and vague and known to cause scruples of conscience to many sincere ministers of moderate theological opinion. It was felt that a short statement of fundamental doctrines would prove to be a more positive approach.

The Panel's proposals were sent down to presbyteries for consideration and comment.

1. *Procurator's Opinion*

While the remit did not mention the Articles Declaratory, it soon became obvious that the proposed measures would necessitate the amendment of these Articles. The Panel therefore sought the opinion of the Procurator as to whether it was within the power of the General Assembly to delete the references in the Articles Declaratory to 'subordinate standards' and to the Westminster Confession of Faith as the 'principal subordinate standard', and to approve a new Preamble. The Procurator's opinion is printed in full as an Appendix to the Panel's report to the General Assembly of 1970 (*Reports*, 1970, pp. 180–182). The Panel, however, printed a brief summary in its own report (ibid., p. 173), and the gist of the summary is that the legal status of the Declaratory Articles makes it unnecessary for the Church to take into consideration the recognition of, or status accorded to, the Westminster Confession of Faith in earlier statutes or laws, such as, for example, the Treaty of Union, and that the Church has the power to declare both the status to be accorded to the Westminster Confession of Faith and the sense in which she understands it. Thus if the Church were to adopt the Panel's proposals, she would be acting consistently with the provisions of the Articles. Further, there is nothing in the Articles which would make it necessary for the Church to subscribe for all time to subordinate standards. Finally, the Church has the power to approve a new Preamble.

Apart from the approval of a new Preamble, any such changes would, however, be subject to the special procedures laid down in Article VIII for the amendment of the Articles Declaratory, which require the overture to be approved by more than two-thirds of the presbyteries in at least two successive years. Textual adjustments, based on the suggestions of presbyteries, could be made but, if the overture as transmitted to presbyteries in its final form did not receive the necessary two-thirds' majority, no similar proposal could be transmitted for five years.

While it would not be necessary to follow this strict procedure in the case of an amended Preamble, the Procurator was of the opinion that, because of the close relation of the proposed amendments to the Preamble and the revision of the Articles, the same procedure should be followed in regard to both.

2. *Overture Transmitted to Presbyteries*

Meanwhile, comments from presbyteries on its 1969 report had encouraged the Panel to continue its planned course and a draft, revised in the light of these comments, was transmitted by the General Assembly of 1970, along with a list of questions to both presbyteries and kirk sessions. The Panel was able to report to the General Assembly of 1971 that the response of presbyteries was increasingly favourable and that of kirk sessions overwhelmingly so. The revised proposals were again transmitted to presbyteries for further comment. The 1971 Assembly also instructed the Panel to prepare an overture under the Article VIII procedure on the proposed new Preamble and amendments to the Articles Declaratory, for presentation to the General Assembly of 1972. When this overture was duly transmitted to presbyteries, the matter passed out of the direct concern of the Panel into that of the Committee on Returns to Overtures, though the Convener of the Panel was invited to assist with the presentation of that Committee's report to the General Assemblies of 1973 and 1974.

Regional Working Parties

The Panel was now free to turn to the preparation of the statement of belief for popular use. In reply to an overture from the Presbytery of Glasgow, the General Assembly of 1968 had set up a Special Committee anent the Doctrine of the Church which reported to the General Assembly of 1969 with the proposal that 'the General Assembly remit to the Panel on Doctrine to formulate from the revised Preamble, when approved, a simple statement of belief for popular use', and this had been accepted by the Assembly. While the revised Preamble had not yet been 'approved', it was agreed that work should start on the new statement and the Panel was authorised to proceed, 'taking note of the statement of fundamental doctrines in the proposed new Preamble'.

The Panel did not regard this as one of its normal remits and, instead of setting up a Working Party of its own, proposed that the preparation of this statement should be carried out by representatives of the presbyteries. To facilitate this, it was authorised to set up four Regional Working Parties, based on the University Faculties of Divinity. Each Working Party was allocated one section of the statement and the function of the Panel was understood to be that of collating and editing the work completed by the Working Parties.

The Continuing Debate

Meanwhile, the overture concerning the amendment of the Articles Declaratory and the Preamble continued to be transmitted to presbyteries and gained the necessary two-thirds' majority in two successive years, it being reported to the 1974 Assembly that forty-nine out of a possible sixty-three presbyteries had given general approval. Amendments to the text were made by successive Assemblies, those accepted in 1974 being strictly of a factual or grammatical nature.

The Panel's proposals had proved to be highly controversial and the debate was keenly argued throughout. While an increasing number of presbyteries continued to give the overture their general approval, there were continuing criticisms on matters of detail. Some members supported the proposed changes, feeling that the concept of 'subordinate standards' had outlived its usefulness; others were willing to accept them as an improvement on what they felt was an unsatisfactory *status quo*. Two small but powerful groups opposed the proposals and gained wider support from those who feared that their adoption might lead to a split in the Church. The main criticisms were made on the one hand by those who wished to retain a position of 'Reformed orthodoxy' which they felt was symbolised by the Westminster Confession and, on the other hand, by those of more liberal tendencies who did not wish to have the fundamental doctrines of the Church too closely defined.

In some quarters, there were criticisms of the Procurator's opinion, which was based on the fact that the Church of Scotland Act declared 'that all statutes and laws affecting the Church of Scotland in matters spiritual, in so far as they are inconsistent with the Declaratory Articles, are repealed and are of no effect' (*Reports*, 1970, p. 180), from which it followed that, under the provisions of these Articles, the Church had the power 'to frame or adopt its subordinate standards, to declare the sense in which it understands its Confession of Faith, to modify the forms of expression therein or to formulate other doctrinal statements and to define the relation thereto of its office-bearers and members' (*Art. Dec.* V). The critics argued that to depart from the Westminster Confession of Faith as the Church's principal subordinate standard would be to challenge the provisions of the legislation leading to the Union of Parliaments in 1707 which, they claimed, permanently safeguarded the position of the Confession.

This is a quite fundamental issue, involving points which are still being made (cf. Prof. Lyall's paper — *The Westminster Confession: The Legal Position*). These points have not been tested, and so it would be out of place to argue for or against them in what is primarily a historical narrative. Other points of criticism were such as could finally be settled by the due procedures of the Courts of the Church. This one continues to raise issues which may best be argued by constitutional lawyers and which, if they are ever pressed to the ultimate, may have to be settled outside the Church. What is being challenged is the general understanding that Parliament, in passing the Church of Scotland Act, had recognised the Church's claim to spiritual independence in that, while the Church is by its nature limited in the interpretation of its doctrines to remaining within 'agreement with the Word of God and the fundamental doctrines of the Christian Faith contained in the [Westminster] Confession', it is the 'sole judge' of that agreement (*Art. Dec.* V). The criterion is thus not the Confession itself, but the 'fundamental doctrines of the Christian Faith' contained in it. It is now being suggested that the Church's right of 'sole judgement' in spiritual matters, notwithstanding the terms of the Church of Scotland Act and the Articles Declaratory, remains limited by the legislation leading up to the Union of Parliaments in 1707, an interpretation which raises constitutional questions both of the present standing of this legislation and of the sovereignty of the United Kingdom Parliament. The specific point made by the Procurator was 'that it is idle to consider, for instance, the status accorded to the Westminster Confession of Faith in, for example, the Act of Union, if on a proper construction of the [Declaratory] Articles, the Church of Scotland is empowered to declare what that status is in relation to its belief' (*Reports*, 1970, p. 180).

Another criticism, while granting the Church's power to depart from the idea of 'subordinate standards' and to amend the Preamble and Articles Declaratory, questioned the wisdom of following this particular method. The Panel maintained that this was the method implied by its remit of 1968, that it had never been given a remit to consider any other procedure and that its proposals had been given general and increasing support.

It was further suggested that the use of the word 'historic' implied the demotion of the Confession to the status of a document which once had a meaning but which was no longer relevant. This had not been the intention of the Panel which, following the example of Reformed churches overseas, had intended to stress that the Church of Scotland was both Catholic and Reformed. It should therefore not take its stand on one seventeenth-century document alone but proclaim that both the Catholic creeds and the Reformed confessions were fundamental to its ongoing life.

Finally, there was a feeling that the Church should settle its doctrinal position first and consider constitutional matters later.

The 1974 Debate and its Aftermath

These criticisms appeared to be undercurrents within a general climate of approval but they came to a head during the General Assembly of 1974. During a lengthy debate, the Assembly first made its final adjustments to the text of the overture, after which it was moved as a counter-motion to the overture that 'the General Assembly do not amend the Articles Declaratory and the

Preamble ... and resolve now to depart from this matter'. This counter-motion was then amended by the addition of the *addendum* 'until a new Statement of Faith is accepted by the General Assembly'. On a vote being taken, the amended counter-motion was passed by 292 votes to 238.

While the Assembly had decided 'to depart from this matter until a new Statement of Faith is accepted by the General Assembly', it was immediately seen that the meaning of this decision was not clear in two important ways. What was the 'matter' the Assembly had departed from and what was the 'new Statement of Faith' to which reference was made? It could be held that the 'matter' was the specific question before the 1974 Assembly, namely the overture proposing a revision of the Preamble and the Articles Declaratory. On the other hand, it could also be held to include the statement of belief for popular use which was under preparation and which was intended to be both dependent upon and complementary to the short statement of belief contained in the sisted Preamble.

In coming to its decision, the Assembly had departed from the short statement of fundamental beliefs in the proposed revised Preamble but, by adopting the amendment to the counter-motion, it had also clearly indicated that it was still looking for the production of a new statement of faith, though it had not specifically instructed the Panel to proceed with the preparation of such a statement, nor had it indicated either the nature of the expected statement or its relation to the popular statement of faith. The hour being now late, it was remitted to the Business Committee, in consultation with the Panel, 'to draft a new remit to the Panel on Doctrine anent the preparation of a new Statement of Faith for submission to a later sederunt'.

After due consultation with the office-bearers of the Panel, the Business Committee reported to a later session which agreed to remit to the Panel, '. . . to consider the situation in which the Church has been placed in consequence of the decision reached ... and in particular the implications of this decision in relation to the Panel's remit' on the preparation of a statement of belief for popular use. The Panel gave careful consideration to both the points at issue. What was the 'new Statement of Faith' the Assembly was expecting? The presumption was that it was to be suitable for formal, constitutional use, but was it to be short, suitable for insertion into another revised Preamble, or was it to be long and detailed, perhaps even a new Confession, to which reference could be made in such a Preamble? The Panel was admittedly reluctant to start work on a completely new major remit before completing similar work it already had in hand. Further, while it was agreed that the Panel could certainly prepare a completely new statement of faith, the question was asked whether, in the current state of conflicting theological ideas, one could be produced which was more likely to achieve general acceptance than the short statement of fundamental beliefs from which the Assembly had just departed.

The Panel therefore turned to considering the status of the statement of belief for popular use, work on which was already far advanced and which was the only statement of faith which the Panel had a remit to produce. However, was this popular statement part of the 'matter' from which the Assembly had departed? The Panel concluded that the original remit of 1969 to produce this might well have been sisted but the decision of the General Assembly of 1972 to authorise the Panel to start work on the popular statement had already detached it from its close dependence upon the statement of fundamental doctrines in the revised Preamble. It was therefore proposed to continue work on the statement of belief for popular use, as an entirely separate task, with the intention of producing a statement which could be judged on its own merits. After consultation with the General Administration Committee, the Panel reported accordingly to the General Assembly of 1975 which agreed with the Panel's interpretation and authorised work to continue.

In coming to this decision, the Panel was aware that the statement being prepared would not be suitable for any formal or constitutional use. While the five-year period of delay laid down by the Article VIII procedure did not apply in cases where the Assembly departed from the proposed amendments, the Panel hoped to abide by the spirit of this delay. It estimated that it would take some five years for the popular statement to pass through all its stages and be accepted by the General Assembly, which would then be in a position to consider what particular status should be accorded to the new statement and what steps should be taken to rectify, if still considered necessary, the formal doctrinal position of the Church.

Statement of Belief for Popular Use

The Regional Working Parties were now committed to their task but they found great difficulty in interpreting what had appeared to be an easily understood remit. Nevertheless, they worked out a general answer to the problem of what the remit meant and completed their work by September 1975, so that the Panel was able to start in earnest on its task of editing and collating. It soon became clear, as had been suspected for some time, that the establishment of four separate Working Parties at an early stage of the process had not been a fruitful decision. Each paper had its own merits, but they differed considerably in style, approach and language and would have to be radically cut and edited.

A complete rewrite was considered, but this would be tantamount to a fresh start which the Panel was reluctant to undertake as it would involve scrapping the valuable work done by the Regional Working Parties. The Panel therefore completed what revision it could in the time available and produced what it considered to be a reasonably coherent first draft. The Panel was aware that the statement had certain deficiencies but, as it regarded the statement as one being prepared from work done at presbytery level, the next logical step was further consultation with presbyteries. The draft was therefore presented to the General Assembly of 1976 as a basis for discussion, to be transmitted to presbyteries for comments, from which it was hoped to discover in which way the presbyteries wished the necessary amendments to be made.

This General Assembly produced another keenly argued debate. Some commissioners, apparently not recognising the special status of the statement, criticised it as if it were a more or less finished production by the Panel, but there was more general criticism against both certain doctrinal inadequacies and the nature of the statement itself. From the start of the project in 1968, there had been two points of view, first that a short dogmatic statement of the fundamentals of the faith, suitable for use as a test of orthodoxy, should be produced; the second that what was required was a less formal account of the faith which could serve the purpose of apologetics. Circumstances had led the Panel, supported by successive Assemblies, to produce the second, but it became obvious that many commissioners now wished priority to be given to the first. However, by 331 votes to 241, the Assembly agreed to transmit the draft to presbyteries for consideration and comment.

After considering these replies, the Panel reported to the 1978 Assembly that the statement had not commended itself to the Church at large, the general tone of replies continuing to be critical of doctrinal inadequacies in the statement. These inadequacies could be at least partly explained as arising in sections which had been prepared when the statement was still being regarded as complementary to an agreed dogmatic statement which contained the missing material. The statement thus still bore evidence of its origins in the sisted revised Preamble.

Like the Regional Working Parties, the presbyteries had difficulty in interpreting the remit and came to conflicting conclusions. About a third of them stated that what they wished was a concise statement of the substance of the faith, either instead of or in addition to the popular statement, while a significant number felt that the best answer would be a series of related statements, each designed for a particular pupose. There was a feeling that the decision of the 1974 Assembly had in fact deprived the statement of belief for popular use of its purpose and grounding and that the whole project should therefore be departed from, but the overwhelming consensus was that the Panel should revise the statement in the light of the comments received. The Panel came to the conclusion that this would not be possible: the revision required would be so radical that it would amount to a completely fresh start and the comments received had been so contradictory that there was no clear, unambiguous guidance as to the direction which a revision should take. Experience had shown the need for a fresh, clearly defined remit.

If any guidance could be drawn from the presbytery replies, it would be that, while the need for an apologetic statement in contemporary terms was generally acknowledged, presbyteries were apparently placing a higher priority on a short, dogmatic statement. Yet there was no consensus as to the nature of this statement. Some wanted any such statement to be open-ended; others were looking for a precise definition of points of doctrine as a defence against heresy. In such circumstances, no statement of faith was likely to gain general approval and so the Panel asked the General Assembly of 1978 for relief from its remit.

The 1978 Debate

In 1977, the Presbytery of Angus had overtured the General Assembly to remit to the General Administration Committee to consider what steps should now be taken to clarify the situation arising from the Assembly's 1974 decision. After consulting the Panel, the Committee reported in 1978 that there was no constitutional impediment to hinder any interested party from raising the matter afresh. That Assembly later agreed to release the Panel from its remit to produce a statement of belief for popular use, with two significant *addenda*. The first was to refer the Church to the first of the Articles Declaratory 'as an authoritative guide in any statement of Christian belief'. The second was to remit anew to the Panel 'to consider the status of the Westminster Confession of Faith as the Church's subordinate standard, and to report to a future General Assembly with, if so advised, new proposals anent the definition of the Church's doctrinal standards'. With this new remit, the Panel was for the first time empowered to consider what steps should best be taken to remedy what had become a very confused situation.

THE WESTMINSTER CONFESSION IN THE PRESBYTERIAN CHURCH OF ENGLAND

John M. Ross

Although the Westminster Confession was drawn up in England, there is not much evidence that it was regarded as the authoritative doctrinal standard by the English Presbyterian Churches which survived the Act of Uniformity of 1662 and were tolerated after 1689. In the great 'subscription controversy' of 1719 the test put to Presbyterian ministers was whether they would subscribe the first of the Thirty-Nine Articles of the Church of England and the answers to the fifth and sixth questions in the Westminster Shorter Catechism. It may be that the Westminster Confession featured in the trust deeds of eighteenth-century congregations, particularly those of Scottish origin, but no research seems to have been done on this matter.

When the Presbyterian Church in England was formed in 1836, the constituting Convention at Manchester resolved to 'adopt, in the fullest and most unqualified manner, the Westminster standards as received by the Church of Scotland, in doctrine, discipline, government, and worship'. At the reconstitution of the Church in 1844 the Synod (the supreme court of the Church, not termed 'General Assembly' until 1921) required all ministers at ordination or induction to declare that they 'sincerely own and believe the whole doctrines contained in the Westminster Confession of Faith ... to be founded upon the Word of God' and to acknowledge the same as the confession of their own faith. A similar declaration was required from elders and deacons.

In 1876, when this Church united with the English Synod of the United Presbyterian Church, the formula was modified to read as follows:

> Do you sincerely receive and adopt the doctrine of the Westminster Confession of Faith as in accordance with the teaching of Holy Scripture; and do you consent to the said Confession as the Standard by which your teaching in this Church shall be judged: it being understood, in reference to the teaching of this Confession of Faith regarding the duty of Civil Rulers, that, while holding the subjection of such rulers, in their own province, to the authority of the Lord Jesus Christ, you are not required to accept anything in that document which favours or may be regarded as favouring intolerance or persecution?

The account given by Professor John Cairns of 'The Doctrine of the Presbyterian Churches', which forms the first chapter of the memorial volume of the 1876 union, relies heavily on the Westminster Confession.

The Book of Order approved by the Synod in 1882 stated the Standards of the Church as follows:

> (*a*) The Word of God contained in the Scriptures of the Old and New Testaments is the only rule of faith and duty.
>
> (*b*) The Westminster Confession of Faith and the Larger and Shorter Catechisms are the Standards of this Church.
>
> (*c*) In subscribing the said Standards, the Office-bearers of the Church, while holding the subjection of Civil Rulers ... are not required ... (etc., as above).

Soon, however, doubts were felt about the adequacy of the Westminster documents as expressions of the Christian faith, and in 1886 the Synod approved a Declaratory Statement of the sense in which the Church understood and accepted the Westminster Confession. This Statement affirmed the love of God for all mankind and the responsibility of every individual for his acceptance or rejection of the Gospel offer. Further, in 1890 the

Synod approved 'Twenty-four Articles of the Faith', newly composed by its special Committee, 'as a statement of the fundamental doctrines held and taught by this Church'. In 1892 the question put to ministers at ordination and induction was altered to read as follows:

> Do you sincerely own and believe, as in accordance with Holy Scripture, and will you faithfully teach, the body of Christian doctrines set forth in the Westminster Confession of Faith and the other Subordinate Standards of this Church, and now more briefly expressed in the XXIV 'Articles of the Faith', approved by the Synod of 1890?

The same question was to be put to elders, with the omission only of the words, 'and will you faithfully teach'. A simpler question was to be put to deacons, without any reference to the Westminster Standards.

The Church did not long remain satisfied with this modification. In 1914 a new formula was approved; the reference to the XXIV Articles was dropped, and the following new question substituted:

> Do you accept the Westminster Confession of Faith and the Larger and Shorter Catechisms as the Subordinate Standards of this Church, believing the substance of the Christian Faith therein contained; and do you consent that by these Standards, constitutionally interpreted by the Courts of the Church, your relation to this Church shall be determined?

In 1921 all reference to the Westminster Standards was removed from the question put to elders.

From 1926 onwards various overtures came before the General Assembly on the relation of the Church to its Subordinate Standards. Eventually in 1942 the Assembly decided to set up a special Committee on the Church's Doctrine, Standards, and Witness to the Faith. This Committee published in 1944 a Study Outline ('What is the Christian Faith?'), designed to promote study of the Westminster Confession throughout the Church, and two Occasional Papers, one by J. M. Ross, a lay member of the Committee, discussing the need for subordinate standards and the Church's relation to them and to Scripture; the other by the Committee's Convener, Professor H. H. Farmer, entitled 'The Westminster Confession after 300 Years' and examining the adequacy of that document as a statement of faith for the twentieth century. At the same time a new edition of the Confession, which was out of print, was placed on sale. The Committee's report to the Assembly of 1945 seriously questioned the value of a system under which ministers had to assent to the substance of the faith contained in a document three centuries old, while the Church had not declared which parts of that document expressed the substance of the faith and which not.

There was tension within the Committee between the view that the Confession was substantially sound and ought to be continually used as a manual of doctrine, and the view that it ought to be replaced by an entirely new statement for current use. In spite of the Committee's attempt to get people to read and study the Confession, in practice it has been very little read or used by English Presbyterians in the present century. The Committee therefore turned its attention to the preparation of a new Statement of the Christian Faith, which was eventually approved by the Assembly in 1957 'as a declaration for this present time of the Scriptural and historic faith', but at the same time the Assembly reaffirmed the Church's constitutional relationship to its Supreme and Subordinate Standards. In practice this Statement has been no more used than the Westminster documents. It has long been out of print.

Meanwhile attention was given to the revision of the ordination formula, and eventually in 1958 the Assembly approved a radical rearrangement under which the Declaration read at ordination and induction services would contain the following affirmations:

This Church acknowledges as her Subordinate Standards the Westminster Confession of Faith and the Larger and Shorter Catechisms, in which her fathers set forth the Christian Faith.

This Church in 1956 accepted a 'Statement of the Christian Faith' as a declaration for this present time of the Scriptural and historic faith, and authorised its use in the teaching of that faith.

D

The ordinand was then merely asked to affirm his belief in the Trinity and in the Gospel of God's grace, preceded by the following question:

Do you assent to this Declaration of the doctrine and practice of the Presbyterian Church of England; do you undertake to exercise your ministry conformably to it; and do you consent that, in accordance with this Declaration, constitutionally interpreted by the Courts of this Church, your relation to this Church shall be determined?

In 1972 the Presbyterian Church of England united with the Congregational Church in England and Wales to form the United Reformed Church in England and Wales. The Westminster Confession and Catechisms have no status as doctrinal standards of that Church. The Basis of Union, after briefly setting out the fundamental doctrines held in common by the uniting Churches, added (in article 7.18):

At the same time the United Reformed Church accepts with thanksgiving the witness borne to the Catholic faith by the Apostles' and Nicene Creeds. It recognizes as its own particular heritage the formulations and declarations of faith which have been prepared from time to time by Congregationalists and Presbyterians in which they have stated the gospel and sought to make its implications clear.

A footnote explains:

E.g. the Westminster Confession, 1647; the Savoy Declaration, 1658; A Statement of the Christian Faith, 1956 (Presbyterian Church of England); A Declaration of Faith, 1967 (Congregational Church in England and Wales).

The statement to be read at all ordination and induction services includes an acknowledgement in the above terms ('The United Reformed Church accepts ... implications clear.'), but ministers are not required to state their relationship to any particular creed, confession, or statement. In practice in the United Reformed Church the Westminster documents, like the Savoy Declaration, are of purely historical interest. When any new doctrinal formulations are required they are constructed afresh.

The reason why the Presbyterian Church of England felt the need of a Subordinate as well as a Supreme Standard is that if Scripture is declared to be the sole authority the door is opened to heretical and subversive teaching based on a perverse interpretation of selected texts of Scripture. The Bible contains such variety of doctrinal attitudes and implications that it can be used in support of almost any doctrine. By contrast the Westminster Confession is clear and unified; but unfortunately it deals only with the matters considered important in the seventeenth century and does not treat satisfactorily of the great doctrinal and ethical issues of the present day; indeed some of its statements would be generally considered in the United Reformed Church as simply mistaken. The Presbyterian Church of England was unable to produce any alternative which could be accepted as a substitute for the Westminster documents. And so for the last century of its existence that Church formally accepted them as its Subordinate Standards but in practice did not use them.

THE WESTMINSTER CONFESSION IN THE PRESBYTERIAN CHURCH IN IRELAND

Revd Professor John Thompson

The Presbyterian Church in Ireland holds the Word of God contained in the Scriptures of the Old and New Testaments to be the supreme standard of faith and practice, and accepts the Westminster Confession of Faith and the Larger and Shorter Catechisms as the subordinate standards of the Church. The Code of the Church, revised in 1979 and published in 1980, states under Section 3, paragraphs 12–14 (p. 10):

The Standards of the Church

12. *The Presbyterian Church in Ireland*, as a witness for Christ, has adopted subordinate standards in which is set forth what she understands the Word of God to teach on certain important points of doctrine and worship. These subordinate standards are a testimony for truth and against error, and serve as a bond of union for members of the Church.

13. *The Confession of Faith* (as approved by the Church of Scotland in her Act of 1647) and the Larger and Shorter Catechisms, prepared by the Westminster Assembly of Divines, are the subordinate standards of the Presbyterian Church in Ireland. Accepting these subordinate standards, the Church holds that, although civil rulers are bound to render obedience to Christ in their own province, yet they ought not to attempt in any way to constrain men's religious beliefs, or invade the rights of conscience.

14. *In the Church* resides the right to interpret and explain her standards under the guidance of the Spirit of God.

The section in paragraph 13 which speaks of civil rulers is intended to qualify acceptance of the Confession, and to emphasise the spiritual independence of the Church under the Lordship of Jesus Christ.

At each licensing of a student, and at the ordination and installation of ministers and elders, this statement is read and questions are put to the candidates with the following form of Subscription:

> I believe the Westminster Confession of Faith as described in the Code, chapter 1, paragraphs 12–14, to be founded on and agreeable to the Word of God and as such I subscribe it as the Confession of my faith.

There is one exception to this general rule. In congregations of the former Munster Presbytery the minister-elect is invited to make a declaration of his faith according to the standards of the Church by personally writing out and presenting for retention among the records of the Presbytery a declaration of his acceptance of the Confession, but not actual Subscription to it.

The present formula of Subscription is similar to that which has been in existence for almost two centuries, but is not without ambiguities and uncertainties (as indeed have been all forms in our history). In recent times this has been seen in the following ways.

1. In 1968 the General Assembly resolved 'that, in view of certain ambiguities and uncertainties regarding the meaning of Subscription to the Westminster Confession of Faith, the Assembly direct the Judicial Commission to consider the manner in which the Church is legally bound to the detailed text of the Westminster Confession, and other related legal matters, and report'. As a result of these enquiries it was discovered that the Church was legally bound by Act of Parliament in 1690 without any qualifications rather than (as had hitherto been supposed) by the Act of Assembly in 1647 and the Act of Union of 1840. This meant that Subscription in the terms above has no legal authority. An attempt was made to rectify this by submitting Declaratory Articles to the General Assembly so that an Act of Parliament could be passed to gain spiritual independence for the Church. However these Articles Declaratory were not accepted by the Presbyteries in sufficient numbers to warrant proceeding further and the proposal for legislation had to be dropped. There was also underlying this attitude a fear that vital doctrine might be jeopardised. The position therefore at present is that the Subscription to the Westminster Confession in doctrinal terms does not tally with the legal position. The Church is bound in law to the totality of the Confession but its doctrinal Subscription has qualifications.

2. In 1974 the General Assembly issued a brief statement of Faith and Order for the guidance of office-bearers and Church members in which, *inter alia*, it was stated:

> It is not surprising that a document of such length and such detailed theological statement as the Westminster Confession should give rise to difference of opinion on less central matters and difference of interpretation on some major matters; and be felt by later ages at some points not to attain to the balance of the total biblical witness.
>
> The Church therefore in practice has allowed a wide liberty of interpretation in matters which do not enter into the substance of the faith. To insist that every sentence contained in the Confession is essential to the integrity of the Reformed faith would divide the Church into innumerable fragments. What the Confession offers is a system of doctrine. It is this system as a series of related fundamental doctrines which the office-bearers of the Church are expected to affirm as a statement of their faith.

Thus it seemed that it was a certain (undefined) system of doctrine contained in the Confession which was subscribed, and not the Confession *per se* — though it should also be stated that the term 'system of doctrine' nowhere appeared in any Subscription formula.

3. In 1979, however, such an interpretation was incorporated into the new Code as follows:

In subscribing these standards, therefore, you solemnly ratify your already declared adherence to this system of doctrine and discipline held by the Presbyterian Church in Ireland.

This section was however deleted in 1980 on at least two counts. On the one hand, what is subscribed is the Westminster Confession alone and not the Catechisms (which are 'accepted'); and secondly, a 'system of doctrine' is nowhere defined but is simply assumed. The same General Assembly agreed to ask the Doctrine Committee to examine afresh the meaning of Subscription to the Westminster Confession.

The nature of the Westminster Confession and the past history of our use of it lead one to expect no great change. In other words, the ambiguities and uncertainties remain, and are likely to do so. What is subscribed is therefore essentially the Westminster Confession as embodying the fundamental doctrines of the faith particularly as they are understood within the Reformed tradition. This is the closest that one can come to a precise understanding of Subscription.

In practice the Confession is taught as part of the course for students for the ministry in Systematic Theology in Union Theological College. Some ministers in Ireland make use of it in Bible classes and mid-week meetings, but over wide areas it is both little known in detail and not much used. However a revived confessionalism allied to an ultra-conservative theology carries the danger of exalting the Confession (more than it itself intended) as almost the only true interpretation of Scripture. Moreover within the Irish context the anti-Roman emphases in the Confession are sometimes used by those who are against the Presbyterian Church in Ireland to affirm (wrongly) that it does not adhere to its subordinate standards.

Furthermore, the history of the use of the Confession indicates a great variety. In the early days from its adoption by the Church of Scotland to the end of the seventeenth century it was understood in the same way as in the Church of Scotland. Acceptance of it was expected but not demanded. In the eighteenth century Subscription was introduced and faithfulness to the teaching of the Confession was a matter of Church Law — albeit honoured more in the breach than in the observance. In the nineteenth century a controversy arose over non-subscription which eventually led to the more serious matter of Arian doctrine within the Synod of Ulster, denying the divinity of Christ. Subscription was required as a test of orthodoxy on the Person of Christ and on the Trinity, and victory on this was gained by the dominant Henry Cooke over his rival Henry Montgomery. An attempt in 1927 to alter the formula of Subscription was unsuccessful. In general it can be said that, despite the ambiguities and uncertainties, the Westminster Confession plays an important part in the Presbyterian Church in Ireland, and has still a profound influence on the faith and life of the Church, in particular in Northern Ireland.

THE WESTMINSTER CONFESSION IN AMERICAN PRESBYTERIANISM

Revd Professor John H. Leith

The influence of the Westminster Confession and Catechisms in the shaping of American life has been very great. Sydney Ahlstrom in a highly regarded history of religion in America has estimated that three-fourths of the American people in 1776 had been significantly influenced by the Puritan and Reformed type of Protestantism. He goes on to say that the influence of the Westminster Assembly on the creative religious movements of the frontier 'defies calculation'.[1] In the years since the Second World War, however, the influence of the Westminster Confession and Catechisms has radically waned.

English-speaking Presbyterians and Congregationalists used the Confession and the Catechisms as their primary theological standards. The Congregationalist Synod of Cambridge, Massachusetts, adopted the Westminster Confession in 1648 with exceptions as to Church government and discipline. The Presbyterians who had used the documents from the beginning made them the official standards of the Church in the Adopting Act of 1729. The Shorter Catechism was used as a text in New England schools and as the basic text for Christian education by Presbyterians. The Baptists also made use of the Confession as adopted with modifications in London in 1677 and by the Baptist Association which met in Philadelphia in 1742. The pervasive influence of the Westminster Assembly continued in American Protestantism throughout the nineteenth century.

1. Sydney Ahlstrom, *A Religious History of the American People.* New Haven: Yale University Press, 1972, pp. 350, 453.

The modern era in interpreting the Confession had its beginning in the controversy concerning Scripture which erupted in the 1880s. This debate was sharply focused in the pages of the *Presbyterian Review* (1880–1889), which was edited by Charles Briggs of Union Theological Seminary (New York) and A. A. Hodge and Benjamin B. Warfield of Princeton Theological Seminary. Briggs welcomed the critical historical study of Scripture. In reaction to these developments, Hodge and Warfield defended a doctrine of the inerrancy of the original manuscripts when interpreted in their natural and intended sense, to which they gave classic expression in an article 'Inspiration' published in the April 1881 issue of the *Presbyterian Review*. In this debate concerning the Bible, Briggs as well as Hodge and Warfield appealed to the Westminster Confession. Briggs contended that Hodge and Warfield interpreted the Confession in terms of the theology of Turretin and not in terms of the writers' intention. ('Documentary History of the Westminster Assembly', *Presbyterian Review*, January, 1880; *Whither?* (1889); *How Shall We Revise the Westminster Confession of Faith?* (1890).)

Warfield argued in detailed studies that the Confession supported his view of inerrancy. (*The Westminster Assembly and Its Work* (1931).) In retrospect it is clear that Briggs and Warfield were alike trying to answer questions that had been precipitated by the development of the critical historical methods of the nineteenth-century questions, which the writers of the Westminster Confession never faced and concerning which no definitive answer could be gained from the Confession.

Two good consequences did follow this debate. First, Briggs collected the works of the writers of the Confession to support his cause. As a result the McAlpine Library of Union Theological Seminary (New York) is an unusually fine collection of Puritan literature. A second consequence was renewed study of the Confession in its historical setting. Briggs himself was a leader in publishing articles on the Confession which seriously investigated what writers of the Confession actually said. He was convincing in his argument that the conservatives in particular read the Confession in the light of their newly developed orthodoxy, though he was apparently not so aware that the writers of the Confession never faced his questions.

The desire to revise and also to replace the Confession likewise contributed to a new interest in it. Again, Charles Briggs was in the forefront in advocating a revision, the central theme of his book *Whither?*. In 1903 the Presbyterian Church in the U.S.A. (PCUSA) made minor revisions; adopted two additional chapters, 'Of the Holy Spirit' and 'Of the Love of God and Missions'; together with a Declaratory statement giving 'an authoritative interpretation' of chapter III on the decrees of God, and of chapter X.iii on the salvation of infants. These revisions, which were acceptable to the conservatives, did not in the end make the Confession a satisfactory contemporary statement.

Efforts to revise the Confession in the Presbyterian Church in the U.S. (PCUS) began in 1935 but only minor changes were finally enacted in 1939. In 1942 two new chapters, 'Of the Holy Spirit' and 'Of the Gospel', similar to those adopted by the Presbyterian Church in the U.S.A., were added. A committee of the Presbyterian Church in the U.S. was appointed in 1959 to study chapter III, 'Of God's Eternal Decree', with the intention of revision, but the committee concluded that the Confession was an integral document and that it was best to let it stand in its historical integrity. The report continued to state that chapter III should be read in the context of the whole Reformed tradition. While these efforts to revise aroused some interest in the Confession in its historical context, the study of the Confession was subordinate to the desire for a new confession.

Neither the study nor the appreciation of the Confession in its historical context became general or widely influential. Conservatives and liberals alike read the Confession in the light of the conservative orthodoxy, the former to accept it and the latter to reject it. These continue to the present to be the dominant attitudes toward the Confession, though there are still signs of an appreciation of its theological excellence and of its constructive rôle in the development of doctrine. This appreciation, independent of liberal–conservative controversies, has also been supported by a few historical studies.

The United Presbyterian Church (UPCUSA), formed by the union in 1958 of the PCUSA with the United Presbyterian Church of North America, adopted in 1967 a new confession, the Confession of 1967, and a Book of Confessions which includes the Westminster Confession (with the revisions enacted through the years by that Church) and the Shorter Catechism along with the

Nicene and Apostles' Creeds, the Scots Confession of 1560, the Heidelberg Catechism, the Second Helvetic Confession, and the Barmen Declaration. In practice the Confession of 1967 is the dominant standard, and the Westminster Confession has a place among Reformed documents.

Within the United Presbyterian Church, however, conservatives still appeal to the Confession as interpreted by Hodge and Warfield. Professor Jack Rogers of Fuller Seminary has cogently argued that this conservative interpretation does violence to the historical meaning of the Confession and to the intention of its writers. Rogers himself studies the Confession and its historical meaning and intends to use it as a guide to theological understanding today.

In the Presbyterian Church in the United States the Confession and the Catechisms (with revisions enacted through the years) remain the official theological standard of the Church. An effort was made (1969–1977) to write a new confession and to adopt a book of confessions, but this endeavour did not succeed in securing the necessary votes.

The Cumberland Presbyterian Church, an outgrowth of the frontier revival of the early 1800s, was born in protest against the teaching of the Confession concerning the sovereignty of God and human freedom, especially the doctrine of predestination. It adopted a recension of the Confession in 1814, and this recension was further revised in 1883.

The smaller and generally more conservative Presbyterian churches including the Associate Reformed Presbyterian Church, the Presbyterian Church of America, the Orthodox Presbyterian Church, the Reformed Presbyterian Church and the Reformed Presbyterian Church Evangelical Synod all affirmed the Westminster Confession and Catechisms as their theological standards. In comparison to other Presbyterians they are strict subscriptionists according to their understanding of the document.

The Confession and the Assembly have been the subject of a number of publications in the past forty years. In 1943 in honour of the three hundredth anniversary of the Assembly, the *Journal of Presbyterian History* devoted its June–September issue to the Assembly. Gaius Jackson Slosser published *The Westminster Assembly and Standards 1643–1652* (1943). In 1951, *A Harmony of the Westminster Standards* was published by J. B. Green. The smaller, conservative Presbyterian churches have produced a number of brief studies designed for church school classes: Gordon Haddon Clark, *What Do Presbyterians Believe? The Westminster Confession, Yesterday and Today* (1956); Gerald Irwin Williamson, *The Westminster Confession of Faith for Study Classes* (1964); Dorothy Anderson, *Bible Doctrine: A Workbook on the Westminster Shorter Catechism* (1954). The Orthodox Presbyterian Church made available through its book services copies of the original text of Confession as prepared by Carruthers and printed by the Presbyterian Church of England. A revision of the Westminster Confession into contemporary English to encourage its use has been published by the Attic Press (1981), and is edited by several ministers and a professor of English.

'The Report of the *Ad Interim* Committee on Possible Revision of Chapter III of the Confession of Faith' to the General Assembly of the Presbyterian Church in the U.S. (1961) contained a summary of the study of this chapter in its own historical setting as well as in the context of Reformed confession generally. Edward Dowey of Princeton Theological Seminary provided a commentary on the Westminster Confession in *A Commentary on the Confession of 1967 and An Introduction to the Book of Confessions* (1968). A widely used commentary on the Confession, *The Westminster Confession for Today* (1960) was written by George Hendry, also of Princeton Theological Seminary. The commentary is a reliable statement of Reformed Theology, but no effort was made to relate it to a historical study of the Confession. Holmes Rolston's *John Calvin Versus the Westminster Confession* (1972), based on a University of Edinburgh dissertation, argues that Westminster distorts in a negative way the theology of Calvin. Rolston's thesis is characteristic of many historical studies which assume that seventeenth-century Reformed theology is a 'fall' from the excellence of Calvin. Such judgments generally fail to note adequately the roots of seventeenth-century theology in Calvin's *Institute of the Christian Religion* or to value properly the necessary rôle that Westminster illustrates in the development of doctrine or the remarkable achievement of the Westminster Confession in the kind of theological excellence to which both Barth and Tillich have paid tribute.[2]

2. John H. Leith. *Assembly At Westminster, Reformed Theology in the Making.* Atlanta: John Knox Press, 1973, pp. 66–8.

John H. Leith, *Assembly at Westminster* (1973) and Jack Rogers, *Scripture in the Westminster Confession* (1967) attempt to study the Confession in its historical context and with an appreciation of its contribution to the development of doctrine. Rogers and Donald McKim also argue in *The Authority and Interpretation of the Bible* (1979) that the conservative doctrine of inerrancy is a serious departure from the teaching of the Confession. Other scholarly studies, not bearing directly on the Confession, but contributing greatly to our understanding of it, include J. R. DeWitt, *Jus Divinum, The Westminster Assembly and the Divine Right of Church Government* (1969); James C. Spaulding, 'Sermons Before Parliament (1640–1649) As A Puritan Diary', *Church History*, Vol. 36, No. 1 (March, 1967); and John F. Wilson's *Pulpit in Parliament: Puritanism During the Civil Wars* (1969).

In summary, three attitudes toward the Confession are easily identifiable. Many conservatives regard the Confession as a perennially valid statement of the faith which can be simply repeated today. An amorphous and mixed group is united in regarding the Confession as out-of-date and of little service today. A third position regards the Confession as an outstanding theological achievement in its historical setting, and values it as an authentic statement of Reformed faith and as a resource for theological work today.

THE WESTMINSTER CONFESSION
IN AUSTRALIA

Revd Professor George S. S. Yule

Australia, unlike America, was a colony of the Establishment — convicts, warders and administrators predominated before the free settlers, and practically none of these left Britain for primarily religious motives. Consequently, the established forms of Christianity were just 'transported' with no thought of change. The English and Welsh tended to be Anglican and Methodist, the southern Irish, Roman Catholic, and the Scots and northern Irish, Presbyterian.

The first colony to be settled in New South Wales was, from a Presbyterian point of view, founded by the Church of Scotland, and automatically adopted its standards. Then came the Disruption, and this too was transported to Australia. This just preceded the discovery of gold in Victoria, which led to a huge influx of free settlers from Britain. Melbourne grew from a village to a city of half a million people in forty years. Here the Free Church influence predominated, but as in Scotland, both the Church of Scotland and the Free Church adopted the Westminster Confession.

There was no commonwealth of Australia till 1901. So each state was sovereign, and each state Presbyterian Church was also independent. Each state assembly adopted the Westminster Confession as its subordinate standard. Victoria, the largest Presbyterian Church, was a special case. Here in 1858 the breach between the Free Church and the Church of Scotland had been healed (with only a handful of congregations staying out). This was the first Scots Presbyterian church to heal this rift. It adopted not only the Westminster Confession but all the Westminster Assembly documents as binding on its ministers.

In 1901, along with the founding of the Commonwealth, came the formation of the Presbyterian Church of Australia. This was a federal union of the state churches, but among other things the General Assembly of the Presbyterian Church of Australia was given sole jurisdiction of doctrinal standards and adopted the Westminster Confession with a Declaratory Act. This allowed liberty of conscience in those matters that do not enter into the substance of the faith, and gave the Assembly the right to determine what these matters could be in any given case. In the late nineteenth century the issues this safeguard was aimed at were predestination to damnation, and, as there was no established church in Australia, those clauses of the Confession that bordered on Church/state relations.

That was the official position and each minister (and until 1923 each elder also) at ordination had to give his assent to the Confession. This still pertains in the Continuing Presbyterian Church in Australia.

As a matter of fact, the theology of the Confession played less and less part in the ongoing life of the Church. Till the 1930s the Shorter Catechism was widely used in Sunday schools and this had quite an effect; but few ministers or lay people seriously studied the Confession. However, when serious cases of heresy arose, as in the case of Professor Angus in New South Wales — 1930–1940 — then it was invoked and used as a safeguard to defend the orthodoxy of the Church.

Then came the move for Church union, whose opponents tended to appeal afresh to the Confession. I should judge that during the controversy over union more people studied it than had done so for many years, but it is not a document which stirred the emotions of many pragmatic Australians, though some used it for pragmatic reasons. The main theological effort of the Australian Church was concentrated on union; the Basis of Union of *The Uniting Church in Australia* insisted that unity must be based on the doctrine of justification by faith; and that Uniting Church is committed to seek the fullness of the faith. To this end, the Basis of Union spells out where this fullness of faith must be sought. Primarily it is in Jesus Christ, as witnessed to by prophet and apostle in Holy Scripture, and now proclaimed by word and sacrament; then in the *Apostles'* and *Nicene Creeds*; and then in the Reformation Confessions. It specifically names the *Scots Confession*, the *Heidelberg Catechism*, the *Westminster Confession* and its partial rewriting in the *Savoy Declaration*, and it adds the *Forty-Four Sermons* of John Wesley from the Evangelical Revival. Then it discusses the place of the creeds, and the way in which they are recognised and are to be used is important.

> The Uniting Church enters into unity with the Church throughout the ages by her use of the confessions known as the Apostles' Creed and Nicene Creed. She receives these as authoritative statements of the Catholic faith, framed in the language of their day and used by Christians in many days, to declare and guard the right understanding of that faith. She commits her ministers and instructors to careful study of these creeds and to the discipline of interpreting their teaching in a later age. She commends to ministers and congregations their use for instruction in the faith and their use in worship as acts of allegiance to the Holy Trinity.

> The Uniting Church continues to learn of the teaching of the Holy Scriptures in the obedience and freedom of faith, and in the power of the promised gift of the Holy Spirit from the witness of the reformation fathers as expressed in various ways in the Scots Confession of Faith (1560), the Heidelberg Catechism (1563), The Westminster Confession of Faith (1647) and the Savoy Declaration (1658). In like manner she will listen to the preaching of John Wesley in his Forty-Four Sermons (1793). She will council her ministers and instructors to study these statements so that the congregation of Christ's people may again and again be reminded of the grace which justifies them through faith, of the centrality of the person and work of Christ the justifier, and the need for a constant appeal to Holy Scripture.

This is an attempt to bring these creeds out of a museum and to use them effectively in the Uniting Church to deepen the understanding of the Faith, to enrich worship by making the adoration of the Holy Trinity central, and to help the members and ministers of the Church to concentrate on the basic issues of the faith, so that when the Church is called to the task of writing a confession of faith it will be in a more sound position to do so.

THE WESTMINSTER STANDARDS
IN NEW ZEALAND

Very Revd Professor Ian Breward

The nineteenth-century British debates about the nature of confessional authority and subscription were echoed by Presbyterians in New Zealand, but most of the concerns were met by the passing of Declaratory Acts, very similar to that enacted by the Free Church of Scotland. In 1901, members of the union General Assembly were apparently agreed about the relationship of Scripture and Westminster Standards as this was defined in the Book of Order with the help of the Declaratory Act, which sought to balance unified confession of the substance of the Reformed faith with liberty of conscience and the right of private judgement.

Ministers and licentiates signed a formula accepting the authority of the Scriptures and Confession at licensing, ordination and induction. Elders' ordination vows were less precise, but the clear intention was that the Westminster Standards were to be upheld by ministers and elders as a normative interpretation of the Bible and a condition of holding office. In practice, the rôle of the Westminster Standards in the life of the Church was increasingly marginal by the 1960s, despite the efforts of the Westminster Fellowship to uphold their importance. The contents of the Confession and Catechisms were virtually unknown to many office-bearers, and many ministers regarded these official standards as of historical interest only, with liberty of conscience and the right of private judgement given a rôle that the framers of the Declaratory Act had never intended.

Just what variety of opinion existed in the Presbyterian Church became clear in the heresy proceedings brought against Principal Geering in 1966 and the discussions which ensued. Though the heresy charges were dismissed, the Assembly asked the Doctrine Committee to clarify the meaning of phrases relating to the resurrection of Christ and the Christian hope, for it was clear that the Confession and Catechisms did not cover the precise issues raised. In addition the Doctrine Committee clarified the meaning of the phrases 'fundamental doctrines of the Christian faith' and 'the substance of the faith', defined what it means to subscribe to a statement of faith, and drafted a simple contemporary statement of faith expressing fundamental doctrines.

The 1969 General Assembly approved a list of fundamental beliefs, in terms of the final paragraph of the Declaratory Act, covering the Bible, God and nature, the person of Jesus Christ, the resurrection of Jesus Christ, judgement and the Christian hope. This was an attempt to draw a clear distinction between the official doctrinal position of the Presbyterian Church of New Zealand and private opinions. In addition, it was noted that while it was difficult to define the content and extent of the fundamental doctrines of the Christian faith, such a phrase referred to 'those affirmations of faith essential to the Church's doctrine and life, without which it does not fulfil its calling to be the community of the Lord Jesus Christ, the One, Holy, Catholic and Apostolic Church'. By continuing to use such phrases, the Church acknowledged its continuing responsibility 'to preserve the fullness and integrity of the Christian faith and to proclaim it effectively'.

That also meant facing the meaning of subscription to an ordination and induction formula. The boundaries between personal witness to faith and a recognisably united and catholic public proclamation of faith, with the real authority that comes from sincerely shared commitment, were not clear. The Assembly attempted to draw a careful distinction between the intention of a Confession and conscientious difference about the precise words best used to proclaim the Church's faith.

> Therefore where any minister or office-bearer affirms a Statement or Confession of Faith he is bound by the faith expressed in the Statement or Confession rather than by the precise words themselves.

It will, however, belong to the integrity of every minister or office-bearer who makes such an affirmation that he will seek to enter as fully as he conscientiously can into the faith the words express.

The Church's right to judge as to whether such faith as he confesses entitles him to holding office in the Church, and the procedure to be followed, is sufficiently set out in the Book of Order, Chapters 9–10.

The distinction between the Church's confessional witness to the historic faith of the Catholic Church and the minister's/office-bearer's obligation to enter fully into this, seeks to ensure that the Church's proclamation has a clear public meaning. At the same time it aims to ensure that the Church's common faith is constantly scrutinised and enriched by the liberty of conscience established when men and women are captivated by the Word of God. One further clarification was added to the Book of Order in 1971 — a Statement about the meaning of 'fundamental doctrines'.

One other issue needs note — the rôle of the Westminster Confession in the 1971 Plan for Union and the doctrinal statement of faith proposed for the uniting church. Like similar statements in the negotiating churches, the Westminster Confession had no finality, 'but insofar as they are consistent with the teaching of the Bible and the Creeds, they will enrich the United Church's understanding of its faith and mission'. Though the future of the reunion proposals is uncertain, New Zealand Presbyterians have begun to understand the difference between a church with a confession and a confessing church, when the joy and pain of continually clarifying the boundaries between contemporary faith and unbelief are shared by the whole church as an inescapable part of discipleship. A Presbyterian church which lacks this type of accountability undermines its unity, forgets its past and is irresponsible to the present and the future. Whether this is best done by regular rewriting of the Church's Confessional documents, or by occasional clarifications which are added to the Westminster standards, has not yet been settled.

A PERSONAL VIEW

Revd George M. Dale

The first major point that I make is that a Confession of faith is necessary. 'The Bible and the Bible alone is the religion of Protestants,' said William Chillingworth. However, the Bible is a complex volume of books. We require, therefore, a summary of the doctrines which the Bible teaches, set down in logical and orderly form, so that what the Church believes is made known in adequate compass. For this purpose we have the Westminster Confession of Faith, adopted by our Church in 1647 as our subordinate standard, subordinate, that is, to the supreme standard, the Bible itself.

Some say that such a subordinate standard is unnecessary. In 1969, for example, a Report to the General Assembly questioned the wisdom of having the Westminster or any other confession of faith 'in this period of ecumenical change and theological ferment'. On the contrary, such a period makes a confession of faith not less but more necessary. Intelligent opponents of our faith can see this. One of them, Baroness Wootton, said, 'Our forefathers, T. H. Huxley, Darwin and others had to fight people who had firm convictions and who, if they went down at all, went down with colours flying. Now we are engaged in a subtle and difficult type of shadow boxing, for the people we are now fighting retain their positions in the churches and at the same time express disbelief in the traditional doctrines with which their churches are associated. When you find a clergyman of the Church of England saying that the motto for the twentieth century should be, "The maximum of faith with the minimum of dogma", you ask yourself, "How silly can you get?" How can you have faith in something which is undefined and which is not to be defined because to define it would be dogmatic?'[1]

It is because our Church believes that a Confession of Faith is necessary that all ministers and elders of our Church have to subscribe at their ordination to the Formula, referring, *inter alia*, to 'the fundamental doctrines of the Christian Faith contained in the Confession of Faith of this Church'. As far as a minister is concerned, this subscription both curtails and enlarges his freedom. It curtails his freedom in that he may not teach doctrines which are not consistent with the Confession. It enlarges his freedom in that he may teach doctrines which are consistent with the Confession.

Ministers and elders subscribe with the qualifying clause, stated in the Preamble, that the Church recognises 'liberty of opinion on such points of doctrine as do not enter into the substance of the faith'. This clause echoes the Confession itself, for we read there, 'God alone is Lord of the conscience, and hath left it free from the doctrines and commandments of men which are in any thing contrary to his word, or beside it, in matters of faith or worship. So that to believe such doctrines, or to obey such commandments out of conscience, is to betray true liberty of conscience; and the requiring of an implicit faith and an absolute and blind obedience, is to destroy liberty of conscience, and reason also' (XX.ii). It will be noted, however, that liberty is not to be unrestricted. The liberty given is not licence. It is liberty of opinion, it is freedom of conscience, as tested by God's word. Moreover, as far as those who hold office in the Church are concerned, it is the Church that decides in any case which may arise what is consistent with God's word and what is not. This was made clear in the Free Church Declaratory Act of 1892:

> ... while diversity of opinion is recognised in this Church on such points in the Confession as do not enter into the substance of the Reformed Faith therein set forth, the Church retains full authority to determine, in any case which may arise, what points fall within this description, and thus to guard against any abuse of this liberty to the detriment of sound doctrine, or to the injury of her unity and peace.

1. *National Secular Society Annual Report* (1969).

If the Church is to maintain its credibility it is essential that the Church should act positively through its courts when this 'liberty of opinion' clause is obviously abused. And obviously abused it sometimes is. There are ministers who deny from the pulpit and/or in print such fundamental doctrines as the authority of the Bible, the fallen state of man, the deity of Jesus, his atoning death on the cross, his physical resurrection, a 'hell to be shunned and a heaven to be gained', justification of the sinner by faith, and even the power of the Holy Spirit. Others see this. In his book, *Confessions of a Surgeon*, George B. Mair, who was brought up in our Church but who might be described as a deist, compares the ministers of our Church with the priests of the Roman Catholic, to the detriment of the former. He writes, 'It became increasingly easy to find common ground with local catholic priests, even if I disagreed with their attitudes towards children of mixed marriages or to contraception. ... At least their views were the views of their Church. ... Most of my parson friends had as many doubts as their flock and they had all my sympathy. I found it especially sad that their minds seemed closed to all historical records which did not fit in with their training while the licence which they used to interpret biblical texts or stories was breath-taking in its audacity.'

Very rarely, however, do the courts of our Church act positively even when it is obvious that a minister is abusing the 'liberty of opinion' clause. It is not that the machinery is lacking in our Presbyterian form of Church government to deal with such abuse. In this area, as in so many areas in our Church, it is the will to use the effective machinery which is there that is lacking. It appears that a member of a court has only to hint that to consider charging a particular minister with heresy would be to make that person the victim of a witch hunt, to cause the court to drop the matter like a hot brick. The failure of the courts to take effective action discredits the Church in the eyes of those who are outside as well as of faithful members.

Of course no one wants to see trials for heresy in the courts of the Church. The onus for avoiding them is, however, upon potential candidates for ordination. If he or she decides that it is impossible honestly to subscribe to the Formula, that person should not go forward for ordination. If after ordination a minister finds that he or she has undergone a change of mind and can no longer adhere to that subscription, the way is open to resign. What C. S. Lewis said in *Undeceptions* to ministers of the Church of England, who subscribe at their ordination to that great confession, the Thirty-Nine Articles, as we do to the Westminster Confession, is equally applicable to ministers of the Church of Scotland: 'We never doubted that the unorthodox opinions were honestly held; what we complain of is your continuing your ministry after you have come to hold them.' Some of our ministers have discontinued their ministry because they have undergone a change of mind. All honour to them.

A fact which opens the way to abuse is that the Church has never defined which doctrines in the Confession are of the substance of the faith and which are not. Some argue, therefore, that the Church should do this. Already it has gone some way towards it, but not very far. It has, for example, made pronouncements with regard to the doctrine of fallen man, pointing out that the unsaved sinner may yet be the author of good; to the doctrine of Christ as the only mediator, stating that God's grace may extend to those, such as pagans and infants, who have never heard of Christ; to the doctrine of the civil magistrate, disowning intolerant and persecuting principles. If the Church were to pronounce on the Confession in detail and define its essential doctrines, this might be regarded as acting contrary to the teaching of the Confession itself, with its teaching that God alone is Lord of the conscience, and that 'The supreme judge, by which all controversies of religion are to be determined ... can be no other but the Holy Spirit speaking in the scripture' (I.x). My personal opinion is, however, that in view of recent events the Church should give serious consideration to the argument that it ought to define the essential doctrines in the Confession.

My second aim is to meet some of the adverse criticisms of the Confession as space does not permit me to consider the Confession itself in detail.

The Confession has been criticised on the ground that it is 'rather man-centred'.[2] As I see it, it is God-centred, in contrast to much theology today which is humanistic. Professor J. S. Whale records in *Christian Doctrine* that a young curate once called on

---

2. *The Westminster Confession.* By the Committee on Adult Christian Education.

William Stubbs, Bishop of Oxford, to ask for advice about preaching. The great man was silent for a moment and then replied, 'Preach about God; and preach about twenty minutes.' The Confession teaches about God, first and foremost, in relation — of course — to his creation and man's place in that creation.

It is significant that the first chapter is entitled 'Of the Holy Scripture', for the Christian religion is a revealed religion and the Holy Scripture is the record of that revelation. 'The whole counsel of God, concerning all things necessary for his own glory, man's salvation, faith, and life, is either expressly set down in scripture, or by good and necessary consequence may be deduced from scripture' (I.vi). I have heard the Confession criticised on the ground that its authors' understanding of Scripture was very different from ours. It was not very different from mine, or that of many known to me.

Of chapter three, 'Of God's Eternal Decree', James Philip stated in his erudite and popular lectures given in 1966 that it is 'probably the most difficult section of the whole Confession'. Certainly it is the chapter most often picked on by those who are antagonistic to the Confession. It deals with the sovereignty of God in man's salvation or condemnation as the case might be. This chapter must be studied in the light of the previous one, chapter two. In that chapter, emphasis is placed on the greatness and majesty of God; but no less emphasis is placed on his graciousness and mercy. The sovereignty, then, is the sovereignty of him who is Father, Son and Holy Spirit, who is 'most loving, gracious, merciful, long-suffering, abundant in goodness and truth' (II.i). This is the nature of him who has 'predestinated unto life' some (III.iii) and, with regard to the rest of mankind, 'was pleased, according to the unsearchable counsel of his own will, whereby he extendeth or witholdeth mercy as he pleaseth, for the glory of his sovereign power over his creatures, to pass by, and to ordain them to dishonour and wrath for their sin' (III.vii). Professor Donald MacLeod's comment on this chapter and section in *The Westminster Confession Today* is illuminating: 'Election is sovereign, reprobation is judicial. ... The elect are chosen sovereignly, but the non-elect are not condemned sovereignly. They are condemned for their sin.' I would also draw attention to what is said in the Free Church Declaratory Act of 1892, but which does not appear to be well known: 'That this

Church does not teach, and does not regard the Confession as teaching, the fore-ordination of men to death irrespective of their own sin.'

Other criticisms of the Confession that I have read are as follows.

One is the somewhat sarcastic comment that the authors of the Confession wrote with 'enviable certainty'.[3] And why not? Surely the Christian is certain and should express Christian doctrine with certainty? Sir Frederick Catherwood has said, 'What people want from a Church in this uncertain world is certainty. It is the churches which speak with the voice of certainty which are full. This is particularly true of the young.' The Church should speak with certainty not because people want it, but because it has it.

Another is that the authors were over-precise, unduly legalistic, and 'dogmatic about mysteries which are beyond the comprehension of finite and sinful men'.[4] Certainly the Confession is precise and legalistic; it would have no value if it were not. It is not too much so. It is dogmatic about mysteries which are beyond the comprehension of finite and sinful men, such as the Last Judgment, because they have been revealed by God and recorded in the Scriptures.

Another is that it is written in theological language which is no longer readily understood. Theology has a language which has to be learned, just as philosophy, architecture, computer science and other branches of study have. It is one of the duties of the Church to teach the meaning of theological terms. I am not convinced that the minister was making things any clearer for his hearers when he said in a broadcast, 'Many do not understand if told they are sinners, but to say that a man is lacking in purpose and needs to be fully integrated has meaning for him.' I also think this mixes up the languages of psychology and theology. We must speak and teach the latter.

Another is that it is wrong to describe the Pope as 'that antichrist, that man of sin' (XXV.vi). Certainly this description has to be seen in its historic perspective. At the same time, such papal claims as that of Infallibility are as unscriptural and unfounded and absurd today as papal pretensions in 1647.

---

3. Ibid.
4. Panel on Doctrine *Report* to 1969 General Assembly.

Of course we recognise that the Confession is not perfect. Some of the Scripture references are inadequate supports for the doctrinal statements to which they are attached. The Confession reflects, to a minor extent, 'the limitations and concerns of the age in which it was drafted'.[5] Yet even one of its critics has written of its 'real qualities of clarity, scriptural precision, and lucid theological statement which make it, as it has been called, the climax of the classical confessions'.[6]

It should be remembered, too, that the Confession is a strong common bond between us and our fellow Presbyterians in Scotland with whom reunion is to be first and most ardently desired. It forms a similar bond between us and our fellow Presbyterians abroad, where the *Reformed Book of Common Order* is enjoying a ready sale. Numerous purchasers have written to us expressing their pleasure that they have in their hands at last, and are able to use, a book which is true to their and our subordinate standard as well as to the Scriptures.

Professor MacLeod of the Free Church of Scotland College has written in *The Westminster Confession Today* of the Reformed Confessions and of the Reformers, 'They were not inherently authoritative, nor were they meant to be regarded as being above revision or improvement. This did not mean, of course, that they would amend them to suit every whim of men or every change of theological fashion. But they were prepared to modify them immediately if it could be shown that they were un-Biblical in any particular. Those of us today who are deeply committed to the Westminster Confession must be careful to maintain the same attitude.' That is my opinion too.

Meantime, I think that the General Assembly was wise to follow the lead of the Very Revd Dr Andrew Herron in 1974: that we should retain the Westminster Confession until we have a new, and better one. The prospect of any such appears to be distant in the light of the history in recent years of doctrinal statements. In 1963 the findings of the Special Commission on Baptism were only received and noted. In 1965 the attempt to re-examine and

5. Ibid.
6. *The Westminster Confession.* By the Committee on Adult Christian Education.

re-formulate the Doctrine of Ordination to the Holy Ministry ended in failure. In 1967 the Statement of the Eldership was no more successful. The document, 'Worship and the Sacraments', sent down to presbyteries in 1975, has apparently sunk without trace. The Statement of Belief for Popular Use was abandoned in 1978 in favour of the existing statement in the First Article Declaratory. In view of the unhappy fate of these doctrinal items, it does not seem likely that we could reach agreement on a complete system of doctrines. We should be thankful that, for the peace of the Church, we have as large a measure of agreement on the Westminster Confession as we do.

Finally, I am grateful to the Panel on Doctrine for inviting me to contribute this personal opinion, and to the members of the National Church Association who have given me their views on the subject. Though I appreciate that the analogy is far from perfect, I am reminded of the words written by Professor Berkhof when composing his *magnum opus*, *Systematic Theology*: 'The work seemed particularly important to me in view of the widespread doctrinal indifference of the present day, of the resulting superficiality and confusion in the minds of many professing Christians, of the insidious errors that are zealously propagated even from the pulpits, and of the alarming increase in all kinds of sects. It ever there was a time when the Church ought to guard her precious heritage, the deposit of truth that was entrusted to her care, that time is now.'

A PERSONAL VIEW

Revd Dr Douglas M. Murray

Since this is a personal view I thought I would begin by giving a brief account of my knowledge of the Westminster Confession of Faith. During my time training for the ministry at New College in the late 'sixties I did not possess a copy of the Confession, nor do I remember many other students having a copy. The Confession was not required reading nor was it made the subject of a series of lectures, although it was referred to in the course of teaching.

The first time the Confession had to be read was at the end of the divinity course when preparing for Trials for Licence as a minister of the Church of Scotland. The Trials consisted of conducting a service of public worship and then being interviewed afterwards by a minister and an elder appointed by the presbytery. At that time the prescribed reading was four chapters of the Westminster Confession, chapters XXV, XXVII, XXVIII and XXIX, which are concerned with the doctrines of the Church and the sacraments. These chapters are in harmony with the teaching of Calvin and of Knox and show the tradition in which the Kirk stands in these matters. As the minister who conducted my interview remarked, the Confession has a 'high' doctrine of the sacraments, something which has not always been appreciated in the Church. I found these chapters in harmony, too, with my own thinking and I did not find their contents controversial, apart from the reference to the Pope of Rome as antichrist (XXV.vi).

At the Service of Licensing, probationers sign the formula: 'I believe the fundamental doctrines of the Christian Faith contained in the Confession of Faith of this Church.' What are these fundamental doctrines? It was never made clear. No criticism is intended of the teaching at the divinity faculties, or of the examination of students by the Church. But the fact that candidates could be prepared for the ministry without having read the whole of the Westminster Confession shows the attitude of the Church of Scotland to its subordinate standard. The Confession was not considered to be of great importance. Is it not time, then, that it was no longer used as the statement of faith of the Church?

It was only after I had completed my training for the ministry that I became more familiar with the Confession of Faith. I carried out research into the history of the Church of Scotland at the turn of the century. It was the period when subscription to the Confession was being revised. Until then ministers signed the Westminster Confession without qualification as the confession of their faith. And so earlier in the nineteenth century a theologian such as John McLeod Campbell had been deposed from the ministry for teaching, in contradiction to the Confession, that Christ died for all men. I came to appreciate the circumstances in which the Confession had come to be written, and that any statement of faith could be changed to meet changing circumstances and to be in harmony with the Church's changing understanding of the Scriptures. I also came to appreciate the Confession's teaching on such an important matter as the doctrine of the atonement. It is for both of these reasons that I believe the Westminster Confession can no longer serve in a satisfactory way as the subordinate standard of faith of the Church of Scotland.

Any statement of faith is influenced by the circumstances in which it was drawn up and the theological outlook prevalent at the time. The Westminster Confession reflects the reasons for its production and Calvinistic theology as it had developed by the middle of the seventeenth century. Before it was adopted the official doctrinal statement of the Kirk was the Scots Confession of 1560. It is worth comparing the two documents to see how different circumstances helped to shape different statements of belief.

The Scots Confession is not so comprehensive or so systematic as the Westminster Confession. It was drawn up quickly at the time of the Reformation by only six men. It was produced by people who were concerned not so much with the details of theological controversy as with the practical problems which faced the Church at the time. It was written to state the reformed faith and to distinguish it clearly from what were considered to be Roman errors. The Westminster Confession, on the other hand, was drawn up by a large assembly which met over several years. It was part of a plan to unite the Churches of England and Scotland in a Presbyterian mould. Those who compiled it were therefore concerned with constitutional and legal questions. There was also the need by the mid-seventeenth century to distinguish the Presbyterian faith, not only from that of the Church of Rome, but from that of other reformed bodies such as the Episcopalians, and the Westminster Confession was used for this purpose in Scotland during the remainder of the century.

No finality of expression was claimed for the Scots Confession. The Preface stated that the Confession was to be altered if any part could be shown to be contrary to Scripture. It was to be a means of understanding the Bible, not an end in itself. Similarly, with regard to Church government, the Scots Confession did not hold that such forms were laid down for all time; they could and should be changed 'when they foster superstition rather than edify the Kirk' (XX). The Westminster Confession stated, too, that synods or councils of the Church 'may err', and that they were not to be made the rule of faith or practice (XXXI.iv). But in practical terms the Confession came to be regarded as the final statement of the Church in matters of the faith. The Bible tended to be interpreted by the Confession rather than the other way round, as was apparent in the trial of McLeod Campbell in 1831. The courts of the Church were not prepared to consider his appeal beyond the Confession to Scripture itself. Campbell maintained that the Church did not remember its place as a church when teaching was condemned simply for being inconsistent with the Confession of Faith, and not because it was shown to be inconsistent with the Word of God. Similarly, in the case of William Dow in the following year, his appeal to the Bible was refused by the General Assembly because the Confession was held to be authoritative in the Church in matters of the faith.[1]

The principle of the Reformation was *ecclesia semper reformanda* — the Church should be continually reformed in

---

1. Andrew L. Drummond and James Bulloch, *The Scottish Church, 1688–1843*, Edinburgh, 1973, p. 206.

obedience to the Word of God. It never reaches its perfect form whether in the way it is governed or in its expressions of the faith. It is not that the faith changes, but the way in which it is understood and expressed can change and the use which is made of such statements will be different at different times. The Church of Scotland claims the right, in the words of the Preamble used at services of Ordination and Induction, 'to formulate, interpret, or modify its subordinate standards'. But unlike some other Presbyterian Churches it has never altered its official statement of faith.

The Church faces very different circumstances today from those contemplated by the Westminster divines. We live in a country which is only nominally Christian and where those who do not go to church far outnumber those who attend. We are in a missionary situation. We need to emphasise the beliefs which unite us with our fellow Christians as we witness together to the gospel over against the prevailing outlook of the times. We need to concentrate on essential beliefs rather than on those which are peripheral. The period after the Reformation was the era of confessions of faith. Most Reformed Churches produced one. It was the age for distinguishing between different beliefs. What we need to stress today are those fundamental things which we believe as Christians and which distinguish us from the largely non-Christian world.

The distinction between such primary and secondary beliefs was made earlier in this century by Dr H. J. Wotherspoon when the Church of Scotland was considering changing the formula whereby ministers signed the Confession of Faith.[2] He contrasted the creeds which contain these primary beliefs with confessions of faith which contain secondary matters as well. The creeds, he said, belong to the whole Church, confessions to one particular denomination. Creeds unite the Church, confessions show the differences between churches. Creeds are catholic or universal, confessions are local and particular. Creeds are brief, confessions are lengthy. Creeds are positive, confessions can be negative and controversial. It is those basic beliefs which are contained in the creeds which we should emphasise today, not the doctrines which

---

2. H. J. Wotherspoon, *Creed and Confession*, their relation to one another and to the Church, The Macleod Memorial Lecture, 1905, Edinburgh, 1905.

distinguish one denomination from the other but those which mark off the Christian Church from other religions and other philosophies of life. We need a statement of those 'fundamental doctrines' of the faith to which ministers are asked to adhere when they are licensed, ordained, or inducted to a charge. Those doctrines are contained in the Westminster Confession but they need to be identified and stated clearly for the sake of those of us within the Church and for the sake of those outside who look to the Church for guidance.

The Westminster Confession of Faith is also unsatisfactory as a statement of belief because of the prominent place it gives to the doctrine of limited atonement, for the atonement surely lies at the heart of the Christian faith. This doctrine stems from the chapter in the Confession about God's eternal decrees, which says that some are predestined to everlasting life and others foreordained to everlasting death (III.iii). This view is called 'double predestination' because it speaks not only of God predestining some to eternal salvation, as does the Scots Confession for example, but also of others being predestined to eternal damnation. It is worth comparing the Scots Confession with the Westminster Confession on this point as well.

In the Scots Confession the chapter about election is placed between the chapters dealing with the incarnation of Christ and his office as Mediator, and those concerning his death and resurrection. Election is to be understood in relation to the saving work of Christ. It is made in Christ and not by an abstract decree. And the chapter speaks mainly about the work of Christ on our behalf, of his solidarity with the human race, and his sufferings and death for our sakes. In the Westminster Confession, on the other hand, the chapter about election comes near the beginning, after the section 'Of God, and of the Holy Trinity', and before the chapters dealing with the doctrines of creation and of redemption. The work of Christ is interpreted in the light of God's predestination. The benefits of his salvation are for the elect alone (VII.v, vi).

This doctrine grew out of the emphasis upon God's sovereignty in salvation. Redemption is his work from start to finish, it is none of man's doing. The fact that not all men believe, however, must mean that God has decreed that not all should be saved. It therefore follows that Christ did not die for all men but only for

E

those who have been predestined. The doctrine is an example of logic taking over from faith. It is argued, alternatively, that if it is said that Christ died for all men, then that leads to universalism, the belief that all men will in the end be saved. But that would be logic carried to the other extreme. We need to be governed, rather, by God's love as it is shown to us in Christ. The gospel does not follow man's logic.

The doctrine of predestination compresses salvation into one moment or stage — the moment of the eternal decrees — rather than taking account of God's work in history and in the present. There are three 'moments' of salvation which need to be distinguished. There is the love of God the Father for all men from all eternity. There is the love of God the Son and his work on behalf of all men in time and history. And there is the love of God the Holy Spirit by whom we can share here and now in all that God has done for us. This love, too, is for all men, but not all come to share in it; not all men open their lives to the work of the Holy Spirit. And so God loves all men, Christ died for all, and the Holy Spirit seeks to share this love with all men, but not all respond. We can thus hold together God's sovereign grace and the fact that not everyone accepts his love. We can believe that salvation depends from start to finish upon God without being led to deny that Christ died for all.

The doctrine of limited atonement also leads to a most serious lack of assurance. If someone asks whether or not they are one of the elect, what can be said? They cannot be told categorically: Christ died for you. Instead they have to be told that if they believe and show the evidences of election in their lives then they can be sure of their salvation (XVIII.ii). But what kind of assurance is that? The assurance is placed on our own response of faith and obedience rather than on the certainty of God's love. We cannot in the end be assured of salvation if we have to depend on ourselves rather than on God.

It may be said that this belief can be omitted from consideration of the Westminster Confession since it does not belong to the fundamental doctrines of the faith, being one of those matters not entering into the substance of the faith about which the Church recognises liberty of opinion. But if any doctrine is fundamental it is surely the doctrine of the atonement. It is precisely on this point, as to what constitutes that vital core of belief, that we need to be clear. It is too important a matter to be left in doubt. The Declaratory Acts of the United Presbyterian Church and of the Free Church of the last century were more satisfactory than our present position, for they specifically dealt with this doctrine and stated in which sense the atonement was to be understood. But even with these Acts there are difficulties. According to the 1879 Act the doctrine of the divine decrees is to be held in harmony with the truth that God is not willing that any should perish. The problem is that such a belief cannot be held in harmony with the teaching of the Confession. The two are incompatible.

What is needed is a statement which sets out the fundamental doctrines of the faith. It would be difficult, if not impossible, to write another confession of faith, and such a document in any case would include other matters which are not essential and upon which not all in the Church would be agreed. A short statement of faith has been drawn up, for example, by the United Reformed Church in England and Wales as part of the Basis of Union of that Church (Clause 17). It is that kind of statement which we need in the Church of Scotland, but the General Assembly did not approve of such a change when it was proposed some years ago. The problem is still with us and has not gone away.

If it is difficult for the Church to agree to a new statement, might it not be possible to make use of such statements as we have? The Church of Scotland already has a declaration of faith in Article I of the Articles Declaratory of the Constitution of the Church in Matters Spiritual, which were drawn up as a basis for the Union of 1929. This Article sets out the basic doctrines which the Church of Scotland believes as part of the holy catholic or universal Church. It was included in the Articles Declaratory to satisfy those at the time who wished the adherence of the Kirk to these doctrines to be confirmed and who were afraid of a creedless Church emerging in the future if such a statement was not made. It also includes, at their insistence, the formulation of the doctrine of the Trinity which reflects the teaching of the creeds. In spite of the obvious difficulties of such an undertaking the Article was eventually agreed upon. Dr John White, the principal architect of the Union from the Church of Scotland side, said afterwards:

> The doctrinal statement is not fully satisfactory to anyone. But it was the very best settlement that could be arrived at, and it was only reached in a spirit of concession and brotherhood. ... To satisfy everybody, the Westminster Confession of Faith would have had to be rewritten — and the New Confession would have been dotted with asterisks because of a multitude of qualifying footnotes.[3]

The problem of drafting such a statement today would be as great if not greater. There is an obvious advantage in using what has already been achieved.

It was also proposed at the time that Article I should be unalterable in order to safeguard the Church's adherence to the faith. But it was argued on the other hand that the Church should not tie itself to any statement of faith which could not be changed. It was finally agreed that the Church has the right to interpret, modify, or add to the Articles, 'but always consistently with the provisions of the first Article ... adherence to which, as interpreted by the Church, is essential to its continuity and corporate life' (Article VIII). The terms of the first Article are to be a constant factor but the Church has the right to interpret them. The reasons for this provision were explained by John White:

> While the creeds are true, they cannot always be accepted in the minute technical detail that was in men's minds at the time they were composed. ... We have a right from the Head of the Church to adjudicate in matters of doctrine: therefore, the Church has the right to interpret the credal statement in the first Article.[4]

If Article I were used as the statement of faith then its interpretation by the Church would be safeguarded. If it were thought unsuitable for use in this way, since it was originally drafted for another purpose, it could be adapted. It has been adapted for use in the Preamble which is read out at the Ordination and Induction of ministers.

3. Augustus Muir, *John White*, London, 1958, p. 193.
4. Ibid., p. 194.

Whatever statement is used, the Church of Scotland needs to affirm what it considers to be the fundamental doctrines of the Christian faith. These doctrines are contained in the Westminster Confession but it is time that they were stated apart from that document.

A PERSONAL VIEW

Revd James Philip

This paper seeks to indicate why the Westminster Confession of Faith should be retained as the Church's chief subordinate standard. It addresses itself, in doing so, to some of the main grounds on which the Confession is being challenged today.

I

The question is asked: 'Why have a subordinate standard at all? We hold to no creed but Christ. The Bible alone is the religion of Protestants.'

It is as well to be clear as to what this attitude really signifies. It is to change the Church from being a *confessional* body to a *confessing* body. The difference between the two is considerable, and has been aptly crystallised in the American *Presbyterian Journal* (vol. XXXV, No. 4, p. 10): 'A *confessional* Church is known by the confession (and constitution) to which it binds itself, and by which it limits, measures, includes and excludes. It has *standards*, and its programme, preaching and teaching are (at least theoretically) expected to conform to its standards. ... A *confessing* Church, on the other hand, declares its beliefs but is not *bound* by a specific creed.'

To dispense with the Westminster Confession as a subordinate standard, therefore, and to treat it with other creeds and confessions merely as a historical statement of the faith, is not only to assert a historical relativism concerning all confessions, but to effect a change from a confessional Church, bound by a

constitution, to a confessing Church, guided by all confessions but,
bound by none. This is to move away from historic
Presbyterianism, however, and will take the Church of Scotland
out of the Reformed family of churches.

The disavowal of a subordinate standard, on the ground that
'the Bible alone is the religion of Protestants', is to misunderstand
the function of a subordinate standard. And it is odd that the
Reformers themselves, with their *sola scriptura* emphasis, should
have found it necessary to formulate confessional standards,
nearly a century before the Westminster standards, if having a
subordinate standard means encroaching on the authority of
Scripture. In fact, creeds and confessions are necessarily
subordinate to Scripture, and neither the Reformers nor the
Westminster divines ever intended that their Confessions should
take the place or usurp the authority of Scripture. The words in
the preface to the Scots Confession, expressing the determination
of Knox and his colleagues to bring all their teaching to the bar
of the Holy Scriptures, are well known; and they are matched by
a similar statement in the Westminster Confession itself (I.x). It is
safe to say, in the light of such statements, that neither the
Reformers nor the Westminster divines regarded their standards
as having absolute authority or being beyond the need of
improvement, still less infallible. They are binding only in so far
as they are biblical.

Rather, the Reformed confessions were meant to serve as
bulwarks against errors and distortions of the faith, just as, from
the earliest times, all credal and confessional formulations had
this function and purpose. The Church has always found this a
necessary exercise, in its determination to stand true to the
apostolic message committed to it, over and against any denial
or repudiation of it, deliberate or otherwise. The need to safeguard
this 'sacred deposit' makes the concept of a subordinate standard
essential. In the light of our own contemporary theological
uncertainty and confusion, it can hardly be argued that such a
concept should now be regarded as disposable.

Nor is it an argument against a subordinate standard to speak
of it as having a defensive, and therefore negative, function; all
doctrinal formulation has a necessary element of the defensive in
it. The doctrine of the Trinity, for example, was stated by the
Church not so much to *explain* the mystery of the Three-in-One

God, as to prevent wrong ideas being proclaimed as the truth. Its formulation became a necessity to safeguard the integrity of the Person of the Son of God, and the integrity therefore of the gospel itself. Most of the great doctrines of the Christian faith have been grappled with in this way, as A. A. Hodge, B. B. Warfield and others have pointed out; they have been the subject of long and thorough debate, and the Church has spoken emphatically and decisively concerning them, in advancing to an ever clearer understanding of the truth. The formulations of Nicaea and Chalcedon, Athanasius, Augustine, Luther and Calvin, and of the Reformed confessions, represent 'the tried and proved faith of the collective body of God's people'; and it is simply not possible for the Church to abandon them without doing itself irreparable damage. They are not open to question, and they are not negotiable, not because they are infallible — no credal or confessional statement can be — but because they have proved themselves as the expression of the orthodox faith of the Church.

Such a definition of orthodoxy as is thus provided by the Westminster Confession constitutes therefore a standard by which error may be determined and identified and discipline administered. The giving of 'confessional status' to doctrines which Scripture itself regards as fundamental to the faith — the sacrificial death of Christ, his deity, his true humanity, justification by faith alone, the Resurrection — provides a necessary and indispensable guideline and standard with regard to truths concerning which the Scripture does not countenance, and the Church cannot afford, either ambiguity or compromise. In this respect the Confession is incomparably superior to, say, the Apostles' Creed. Who, except the theologically uninstructed, could prefer the Creed's 'crucified under Pontius Pilate' — which is a fact of history rather than an article of faith — to the Confession's statements on Christ the Mediator and on Justification, statements based upon the apostolic interpretation of the fact of Christ's death which makes it a gospel?

II

It is true, of course, as has been said, that no confessional statement is above revision or improvement, still less infallible.

There is nothing inherently authoritative about the Westminster Confession, and nothing infallible about the men who formulated it. In no sense can it be regarded as 'the last word' in doctrinal definition; nor would any of its most responsible advocates, however staunch and dedicated to its teaching, claim this for it. Indeed, if the principle of progress in theology is recognised — and this is really what the aphorism *ecclesia reformata reformanda est* implies — the question of the development, and even revision, of doctrinal standards necessarily arises. Historically, the Church of Scotland's replacement of the Scots Confession by the Westminster documents is a case in point, when it declared that in adopting the latter they were found 'to be most agreeable to the Word of God, and in nothing contrary to the received doctrine, worship, discipline and government of the Church'. It would be foolish to deny that the task of the Church today includes the duty and discipline of making understandable to people of the twentieth century the great, timeless truths of the Christian message, to do this, moreover, for a generation that is theologically illiterate and lacking in the kind of biblical knowledge that could be assumed by the compilers of the Westminster documents.

All this may be conceded; indeed it is surely self-evident. Yet it is one thing to recognise the possibility of some sort of revision or development as a concept, and to acknowledge that a living, vital and crusading Church, sure of what it believed, could no doubt go beyond the Westminster Confession in testifying to the riches of Divine truth; but it is quite another matter to advocate change, revision and redefinition on the ground that 'the Confession is outdated and outmoded, and it just will not do'. This, indeed, is something very different. And it is evident from many statements made during the current debate on the Confession that the motivating reason for such change, and even for departure from it as a subordinate standard, is not that doing so would represent an advance or an improvement, nor that the Confession lacks clarity or relevance, but that there is a substantial disagreement with its scriptural and reformed character. The 'advance' or 'development' envisaged is not a richer and fuller exposition of biblical truth, but a deletion of, and departure from, truths that are no longer acceptable.

The history of modern attempts at revision, such as that

F

initiated in the U.S.A. in the nineteenth century and continued in our time, makes it plain that the result has not been doctrinal progress and gain, such as hoped for by men like B. B. Warfield, to 'develop the structure of the old Reformed theology along its own essential and formative lines in the face of the new systems of error and in conquest over them', but doctrinal retrogression.

But clearer and more precise definition to meet new errors and dangers is not what was in view — neither then nor now. For the changes envisaged today can hardly be described as being 'in nothing contrary to the received doctrine' of the Church. It is here that the advocates of such views decisively part company with the Reformers, who conceived it as their God-given task, not to change and update the ancient confessions of the Church, but rather to restore the Church to the confessional position of the apostles and of the New Testament itself. It is no evidence of the *semper reformanda* principle to initiate the Church's departure from its historic position and its biblical foundations by seeking to establish an irreducible minimum of belief to which the generality of the Church might feel itself able to subscribe. 'An expression of belief currently accepted', as this would represent, is no longer 'a confession of faith'.

St Luke's 'things most surely believed' have tended, it would seem, to become 'things no longer believed', or at the least 'things about which many are no longer sure'. It has, of course, become fashionable to speak of doubt and uncertainty in matters of faith, and it is understandable, since this is so, that the clear and unequivocal note sounding in the Westminster documents should come in for unfavourable, not to say contemptuous, comment. But the quarrel here is not so much with the Westminster Confession as with the New Testament itself. The apostolic message is nothing if not positive, definite and unmistakable. As James Denney puts it:

If we have any gospel at all, it is because there are things which stand for us above all doubts, truths so sure that we cannot question them, so absolute that we cannot qualify them, so much our life that to tamper with them is to touch our very heart. Nobody has any right to preach who has not mighty affirmations to make concerning God's Son, Jesus Christ — affirmations in which there is no ambiguity, and which no questioning can reach.

The Church must make up its mind about this. It cannot have it both ways.

III

But there are those who, while disavowing any radical rejection of the Confession, still nevertheless wish changes on the grounds of the unsatisfactory nature of some of its teaching, which is held to be defective and misleading in some of its emphases, deficient also in some of the things it does not say; and particularly in the scholastic and legalistic tendencies in its theology which have had, it is claimed, a deadening and petrifying influence in the Church's life.

That the Confession is not infallible, and that it is in some aspects deficient, has already been conceded. But the Church is by a long way too uncertain of itself and its beliefs to make the attempt today to rewrite its confessional position — a fact which several attempts in the past few years to do so have made only too clear. And it is therefore very much open to question whether this is a time for redefinition at all, when the real struggle is not for the reformulation of the confessional position in terms understandable to twentieth-century man, but for the integrity of the gospel itself and the preservation of the historic faith. Given the conditions that now obtain in the Church should not our task be to hold fast to what has been committed to us?

One of the ways in which the theological uncertainty is seen is in the criticism sometimes made of the Confession in its alleged one-sided presentation of the doctrine of the atonement, in the emphasis it makes on justification, to the exclusion of the idea of reconciliation. It is true that reconciliation is not discussed in the Confession; true also that the richness of the biblical doctrine of atonement includes more than is expressed in any one statement about it; but if justification is, as Luther maintained, the article of faith by which the Church stands or falls, and if reconciliation itself in the Pauline writings is grounded on the atonement wrought by the justifying mercy of God in Christ Jesus (Romans 5; 2 Cor. 5), it is difficult to see how the Confession's sublime statement on justification can on this ground be faulted — particularly since 'reconciliation' has today become a loaded term, and has been invested with a meaning in socio-political terms very different from its use in Scripture.

It is true also that there is no chapter in the Westminster Confession on the Holy Spirit. In the light of contemporary discussion about the Person and gifts of the Spirit, this places the Confession in a disadvantaged position, and is one area of doctrine where new material could be usefully added. But we must keep this omission in perspective: the doctrine of the Holy Spirit was not seriously at issue in the seventeenth century when the Confession was written, in the way some other doctrines were. This does not mean, however, that the work of the Holy Spirit is set at a discount or neglected; indeed, it is implied constantly as we see from the statements in VIII.vi, and in X, since it is the Holy Spirit alone who effectually applies Christ's redemption to man's hearts. Effectual calling is the direct work of the Spirit of God. Besides, can we really expect the Westminster Confession — or any Confession — to say everything about everything? We must be reasonable. The critical issues in which the faith of the Church is under attack today are not doctrines such as that of the Person and Work of the Holy Spirit, or Sanctification (which has also been criticised as being defective in the Confession) but the Deity of Christ, the Atonement, Justification by faith alone, and the Resurrection — and these are matters that *are* dealt with, substantially and unequivocally.

Finally, something must be said about the charge that the theology of the Confession is scholastic and legalistic, and has had a deadening and petrifying influence on the life of the Church.

It is true that the theology of the Confession represents a development from that of Calvin; but it need not necessarily be assumed that such development is a legalistic and scholastic corruption of Calvin's teaching. It should be remembered that it was the considered view of the Church of Scotland, when the Scots Confession was superseded by the Westminster documents, that the latter were 'in nothing contrary to the received doctrine, worship, discipline and government' of the Reformed Church in Scotland. Furthermore, the fact that the first chapter of the Confession deals with the authority of Scripture is surely significant and decisive evidence that its compilers regarded themselves as being directed and controlled by Scripture in all that they wrote, and that Scripture was the guiding principle in all the Confession was to say.

As to the charge that the Westminster theology has exercised a deadening and petrifying influence on the life of the Church, two things may be said. One is that the Church's practical neglect of the Westminster Confession for most of this century gives the lie to the claim that adherence to it is a force for stagnation. Only someone with little understanding of the Church's situation in Scotland in the twentieth century could suppose that it had been dominated by the teaching of the Westminster Confession, or that that teaching had led to stagnation. It is simply naïve to suppose this, when it must be patently obvious that the reasons for the decay in the Church's life lie in a very different direction, in its uncertainty about the central doctrines of the faith and of the Confession — not the controversial peripherals, but the basic issues of justification, regeneration, the Deity of Christ and the Resurrection.

Nor is the charge of stagnation and petrifaction self-evident in pragmatic terms. It is doubtless true that there are areas in Scotland where forms of near-fatalism and legalism have brought about paralysis; but it is not necessary to assume that this spiritual 'arterio-sclerosis' is due essentially to the Confession. Other, ethnic and cultural, considerations may have just as much to do with it. It is easy to make assumptions; but they fail to account for very different patterns in other places and at other times, as well as in the present day.

There is more than a little evidence in contemporary Church of Scotland situations of a seal of divine approval on ministries that owe their inspiration to the confessional standards; and far from having a deadening and petrifying influence, they show all possible signs of life and vitality, abounding in the liberty of the Spirit, and fruitful to a degree in servicing the Church at home and abroad with men and women of calibre and character. It is an open question whether this indisputable fact has been, or is being, considered with the seriousness it deserves. There are grounds for supposing that it has more to say to the Church than has hitherto been appreciated.

CONFESSIONAL SUBSCRIPTION: A PERSONAL VIEW[1]

Revd Professor John K. S. Reid

1. *History and Theology*

Theology, and the framing of creeds and confessions, are always deeply affected by apparently external and adventitious factors, though this is not always realised or admitted. The Westminster Confession is no exception to the rule. This alone is ground for reviewing it and revising the place it holds in the Church today. In the *Expository Times* (April 1980) I set out the case for radical revision; other contributors to this volume advocate the same course. The same reasons also require revision of the use made of the Confession in the matter of Subscription; and this is the theme to be developed here.

2. *Apparatus of Application*

The half-century following approval by the Church of the Westminster Confession is crammed with events which leave indelible marks on the confessional situation. The theological content of the Confession and its predecessors receives scant attention; instead they come to be tossed about as party badges on the tides and currents of political events. Illustrative of this is the fact that the Westminster Confession did not achieve its

---

1. The writer is specially indebted to G. D. Henderson, Introduction to *Scots Confession* and *Negative Confession*, Church of Scotland Publications, 1937; and James Cooper, *Confessions of Faith and Formulas of Subscription*, Glasgow, 1907, from which several quotations have been taken.

solitary predominance overnight, but only forty years after its initial acceptance: its eventual position (at the expense of the Scots Confession) it owed less to deliberate and responsible theological choice than to hard bargaining with the new monarchy resulting in the 1690 Revolution Settlement — and, one is obliged to add, to sectarian rivalry and even warfare. For the first decade the Westminster Confession gained in popularity with the Presbyterians, but the surviving bishops favoured the Scots Confession; in the next three decades of the 'Second Episcopacy' the Scots Confession recovered the ground it had lost, only to surrender it at the time of the Settlement.

In all this, two earlier developments should also be noticed.

2.1. The concept had been emerging of obligatory adherence to a Confession — first to the Scots, later to the Westminster. This represented a narrowing of both theology and churchmanship: the use made of the Confessions turned them into partisan banners and sectarian badges, and as such they came to be put forward for acceptance or compliance by individuals. The earliest such use is commendably free of the taint of sectarianism: the 1560 'Form and Order' contains Questions to be used in 'election of a Superintendent' and also 'of other Ministers'. The Questions are scriptural and christological, without mention of Creed or Confession. This reticence was soon abandoned. The attempt was made to exact adherence to the Confession itself, and the notion of Subscription was devised, with unavoidable negative, even minatory, overtones. Thus in 1567 the General Assembly petitioned the Scottish Parliament to 'discern [as] no members of the Kirk within this realm' those that should 'gainsay' the Confession. Positive subscription seems at first not to have been demanded of all. But a 'Roman scare' developed: in 1579 we hear of 'Jesuits repairing to this country', and in 1580 of 'Romanists swarming home to Scotland "like locusts"'; and it was commonly believed that papal dispensation enabled and encouraged 'many masked Papists' to subscribe 'the old [Scots] Confession deceitfully'. As response to a situation thought alarming, legislation was invoked; dubious cases were required to 'subscribe the articles of religion previously (1579) established'; and the Negative Confession (1581) was formulated in such terms as the deceit of even Jesuits could not swallow. Legislation was eventually passed (though probably not operated) by which 'all the people was enjoined by State and Church alike' to subscribe it.

2.2. In a second development, a wild flurry of events involved Confession with Covenant in an alliance that politicised the Confession and downgraded its theological significance. The Church had armed itself both defensively and offensively with the Scots and Negative Confessions. The General Assembly deemed the latter to be 'a true and Christian Confession to be agreed unto by such as truly profess Christ's true religion'; and some Roman Catholics at least thought the Church was determined to 'compel all men to swear and subscribe'. But in 1638 arose a need for united national opposition to King Charles's ecclesiastical programme. This was met first by the National Covenant, and then later by the even more political and aggressive Solemn League and Covenant of 1643. The enthusiasm with which the Covenants were signed was hardly theologically discriminating. Signatories endorsed a large heterogeneous package. This included the Scots Confession and the Negative Confession with its many 'detestations and abrenunciations' both of Rome and of Episcopalianism (the Five Articles of Perth) — a rejection which an alarmed Charles, by his clumsy intervention, contrived to render not unacceptable even to many Episcopalians — together with, *inter alia*, pledges to extirpate episcopacy in England and popery in Ireland, and to preserve 'the Rights and Privileges of the Parliaments and the Liberties of the Kingdoms, of the King's Majesty, Person and Authority'. The milder National Covenant, which specifically included the anti-Roman Negative Confession, attracted widespread acceptance. Sometimes compulsion was used to obtain subscription. When this happened, even modern scientific psephology would find it difficult to say how many of those thus coerced to subscribe the Negative Confession were *ex animo* attesting their religious convictions.

3. *The Meaning of Subscription*

Between 1560 and 1690 three questions were being variously answered. Historical events compel the Church to take position, and, in the lack of clear theological direction, this happens haphazardly.

(a) *Of whom is subscription required?* 1560 — Questions are directed to superintendents and ministers only; 1581 and 1638 — subscription required of 'all'; 1707 — after the collapse of the ideal of a single Church within the realm, the Church settles for requiring it of ministers and office-bearers only.

(b) *What is subscribed?* 1560 — 'doctrines contained in the Scriptures'; 1638 — Scots Confession; 1690 — the Covenants having become a dead letter, 'approbation' of the Westminster Confession.

Sometimes there is an accompanying abjuration. So in 1711 we find: 'disown Popish, Arian, Socinian, Arminian, Bourignian, and other doctrines ... whatsoever, contrary to ... the [Westminster] Confession of Faith.' Few today are likely to feel tempted to embrace Bourignianism. But everyone today should learn from its inclusion in official documents exacting adherence how pervasively these are affected by adventitious circumstances, and may draw the further conclusion that they must be subjected to constant review and revision.

(c) *What exactly does subscription entail?* 1690 — 'approbation of the [Westminster] Confession of Faith', which is equivocal; 1711 — 'own and believe the whole doctrine of the [Westminster] Confession of Faith to be the truth of God contained in the Scriptures'; 1690 — the Confession is affirmed as 'containing the sum and substance of the doctrine of the Reformed Churches', but 1692 — 'of the Protestant religion professed in these Kingdoms'. In 1690, 1693, 1700 and 1706 subscription is spoken of 'as confession of their/my faith' (repealed in 1905).

4. *Truths Obscured*

It should not be in the least surprising that the profoundly theological matter of confession and formulae of application should be affected by influences not strictly theological. Theology is never done in a vacuum sterilized from contemporary happenings. Nor was the incarnation so effected. Confession is extorted from the Church by circumstances that oblige it to take action — as Augustine says, *non sponte sed coactu*, not spontaneously but under compulsion. But theology is at the same time obliged to be critical and discriminating about the effect history is having upon it. In seeking and stating the truth that is in Jesus we have as ally the Holy Spirit; and that alliance enables us to be masters of history, if we will, and not mere victims. In the present case, historical events like those briefly mentioned have propelled the Church into a position in which two truths are obscured: the absolute priority of belief in God, and the absolute priority of Scripture over Confession.

4.1.   St Thomas says, *actus fidei terminatur non in enuntiabile sed in rem*, 'the act of believing does not reach its goal in articulation, but in reality'; and a recent Roman Catholic writer virtually translates this when he says, 'I do not believe in the statements of any Creed — I believe in God.' The course of events has kept nudging the Church towards applying its Confessions for partisan purposes. Subscription becomes the attestation of true Presbyterian belief, and the abjuration of Romish or Episcopalian (or Bourignian!) deviations. The Confession has become the touchstone of Scottish Christianity; confession of God has receded into the background.

Belief in God (*fiducia*) and belief of doctrinal affirmation (*assensus*) can of course never be quite separated. If I believe in God, I do not believe simply in the vocable g—o—d: there must be some minimum of connotation. Scripture testifies to this when Hebr. 11:6 says that 'he who comes to God must believe that he is and that he is the rewarder of them that seek him.' Trouble begins when the second element of 'belief that' comes to overshadow the indispensable and prior 'belief in'.

The form in which Creeds and Confessions are cast is significant here. The Apostles' and Nicene Creeds begin with 'I/We believe in God'. and there follows a comparatively brief specification of that in which belief primarily reposes. This balance the sheer length of the Confessions tends to disturb. But even among them there is some difference. The 'we subscribe' required in 1638 of all persons was directed to the Scots Confession, which begins, 'We confess and acknowledge one only God'. Here the priority of belief in God is not lost. The Westminster Confession in contrast contains no such initial affirmation; it launches forthwith into pure theology, 'Of the Holy

Scripture', 'Of God', and so on. The kind of belief subscription to this document implies is quite different from belief in God — as different as *assensus* from *fiducia*; and it is to say the least considerably different from that required in the case of a document beginning, 'I/We believe in God', whether the Scots Confession, the Apostles' Creed, or the Nicene Creed.

On the whole the Church in Scotland has stopped short of pure replacement of belief in God by belief in Confession. Examination of the answers given to 3(c) above reveals some reluctance to require straight unqualified and unequivocal belief in the Westminster Confession alone. Belief in Confession does not quite displace belief in God. But it is quite clear that attention has been mischievously diverted from simple belief in God to things said about God. The belief chiefly, and sometimes alone, required is not that belief in God which alone may primarily be exacted of a Christian, whether private or office-bearing. Today neither the Formula nor the Questions put to ordinand elders so much as mention belief in God! The balance cries out for correction.

4.2. Examination of today's application of the Westminster Confession discloses another distortion. From the start the Confession was accepted by the Church with certain reservations 'as to the truth of the matter' (1647). It is not too much to say that with the provision of reservations the authority of any Confession begins to crumble. The reservations made early on saved the Westminster Confession for the outstandingly important and valuable rôle it discharged in the decades following its adoption. But their multiplication and expansion, e.g. in the Declaratory Acts and Articles, precipitates a situation quite different in principle, though their gradual introduction conceals the scale of the transformation. The centrally important phrase in today's application is 'the fundamental doctrines of the Christian faith'. It is the distillation of a long process which, traced back, leads by way of 'grand mysteries and fundamental verities of the Gospel' (1720 ff.), 'as to the truth of the matter' (1647), and by other similar stages, until 1560 is reached, when the Questions refer to 'the doctrines contained in the Scriptures', together with the acknowledgment of Christ's person and work, defined in Scriptural terms, and the resolve to 'maintain the purity of doctrine contained in the most sacred Word of God'. This bears some resemblance to the apparatus in use today. But there is also this fundamental difference: we are today to find the 'fundamental doctrines of the Christian faith' *in the Westminster Confession.* What can this possibly mean? Various answers can of course be given. But it is difficult to escape the conclusion that the Westminster Confession, so placed, is masquerading as a rule of faith instead of as a rule of thumb. One is led to suspect that we have reached this position by trying to salvage as much as possible out of the historical past, and thus have come to devise this equivocal rôle for the Confession. It is humiliating to history to attempt to shore it up in this artificial way. Certainly cavalier treatment of history seldom pays — it has a way of tactically withdrawing, only to reassert itself at a later time. But moments do come when it is necessary to discard some historical material because it has become burdensome, obstructive and misleading. By returning to the simplicity of 1560 we should be learning from our history instead of continuing to stagger under the burden of it. When their full value is ascribed to the privative qualifiers, 'substance of the faith', 'fundamental doctrines', 'contained in', the relationship to the Westminster Confession at present operating is reduced to ruins. What was a milestone on our way becomes a millstone on our necks.

5. *Conclusion*

The conclusion to be drawn from this study of the apparatus for applying the Westminster Confession is that modification of the present relation of the Church to it is imperative. Of the many and great benefits such a change would confer, two may be mentioned.

5.1. The Church has a continuing mandate to pursue its theological task. This is to be heeded at all times, and at certain crucial moments to be discharged by the formulation of considered credal statements. In reviewing and revising the relationship, the Church will be reminded of this obligation and be freed for compliance with it. There is a certain pluralism within the Christian Church today, a multiplicity of varying and by no means always harmonious views. Those who resist reassessment of the relationship do so with excellent intentions, but the consequences are disastrous. Of course, securely immured and immobile behind the ramparts of a noble but outdated Confession, they can afford to ignore, certainly to deplore, and possibly to fear this pluralism, nervous lest it compel the Church to move. For those who acknowledge theology to be an ongoing task and obligation, pluralism is neither frightening nor daunting: it only makes the task of stating the faith a little more difficult, and at the same time a lot more exciting and necessary. They have no need to be prodded into action: they know the Church must always be on the move.

5.2. The Reformation failed in one important respect: the Christian Church of the West was not as a whole to benefit from its insights. Past history seems to have done its best to make these insights the tenets of the Reformed portion of the Church only, and then to turn them into particular characteristics of the several denominations within the Church Reformed. Today history can be reversed. The Reformers in their best moments knew that the Holy Spirit had led them stumbling to the discovery of more of the unfathomable riches of the Gospel, and realised that they had to hold these further riches in trust until the dawn of a new day of understanding should make it possible to add them to the patrimony of the whole Church. That day has now dawned. The climate created by the ecumenical movement makes it possible for long-separated Churches to share with and to accept from each other the truths of their respective heritages.

From the very beginning, honesty and conscientious scruple forced the Church to supply a great range of qualifications and reservations in defining the tie by which it bound the Westminster Confession to itself. This tie is now badly frayed, and the credibility of the Westminster Confession seriously compromised. The Church should now break that tie, disown the Confession as 'subordinate standard', and honour it so far as it is intrinsically, i.e. scripturally, worthy. Both the Confession and the Church would instantly benefit. The Westminster Confession deserves more honest and honourable treatment than it is at present accorded: placed resolutely in the past, from which it has exercised an influence of crucial but now diminishing value, it would gain a respect enhanced because unequivocal. For the

APPENDIX

Declaratory Act of the United Presbyterian Synod, May 1879

Whereas the formula in which the Subordinate Standards of this Church are accepted requires assent to them as an exhibition of the sense in which the Scriptures are understood: Whereas these Standards, being of human composition, are necessarily imperfect, and the Church has already allowed exception to be taken to their teaching or supposed teaching on one important subject: And whereas there are other subjects in regard to which it has been found desirable to set forth more fully and clearly the view which the Synod takes of the teaching of Holy Scripture: Therefore, the Synod hereby declares as follows:

1. That in regard to the doctrine of redemption as taught in the Standards, and in consistency therewith, the love of God to all mankind, His gift of His Son to be the propitiation for the sins of the whole world, and the free offer of salvation to men without distinction on the grounds of Christ's perfect sacrifice, are matters which have been and continue to be regarded by this Church as vital in the system of Gospel truth, and to which due prominence ought ever to be given.

2. That the doctrine of the divine decrees, including the doctrine of election to eternal life, is held in connection and harmony with the truth that God is not willing that any should perish, but that all should come to repentance, and that He has provided a salvation sufficient for all, adapted to all, and offered to all in the Gospel; and also with the responsibility of every man for his dealing with the free and unrestricted offer of eternal life.

3. That the doctrine of man's total depravity, and of his loss of 'all ability of will to any spiritual good accompanying salvation', is not held as implying such a condition of man's nature as would affect his responsibility under the law of God and the Gospel of Christ, or that he does not experience the strivings and restraining influences of the Spirit of God, or that he cannot perform actions in any sense good; although actions which do not spring from a renewed heart are not spiritually good or holy — such as accompany salvation.

4. That while none are saved except through the mediation of Christ, and by the grace of His Holy Spirit, who worketh when, and where, and how it pleaseth Him; while the duty of sending the Gospel to the heathen, who are sunk in ignorance, sin, and misery, is clear and imperative; and while the outward and ordinary means of salvation for those capable of being called by the Word are the ordinances of the Gospel: in accepting the Standards, it is not required to be held that any who die in infancy are lost, or that God may not extend His grace to any who are without the pale of ordinary means, as it may seem good in His sight.

5. That in regard to the doctrine of the Civil Magistrate, and his authority and duty in the sphere of religion, as taught in the Standards, this Church holds that the Lord Jesus Christ is the only King and Head of the Church, and 'Head over all things to the Church which is His body'; disapproves of all compulsory or persecuting and intolerant principles in religion; and declares, as hitherto, that she does not require approval of anything in her Standards that teaches, or may be supposed to teach, such principles.

6. That Christ has laid it as a permanent and universal obligation upon His Church, at once to maintain her own ordinances, and to 'preach the Gospel to every creature'; and has ordained that His people provide by their free-will offerings for the fulfilment of this obligation.

7. That, in accordance with the practice hitherto observed in this Church, liberty of opinion is allowed on such points in the Standards, not entering into the substance of the faith, as the interpretation of the 'six days' in the Mosaic account of the creation: the Church guarding against the abuse of this liberty to the injury of its unity and peace.

Declaratory Act of the General Assembly of the Free Church, 1892 — Anent the Confession of Faith

Whereas it is expedient to remove difficulties and scruples which have been felt by some in reference to the declaration of belief required from persons who receive licence or are admitted to office in this Church, the General Assembly, with consent of Presbyteries, declare as follows:

That, in holding and teaching, according to the Confession, the Divine purpose of grace towards those who are saved, and the execution of that purpose in time, this Church most earnestly proclaims, as standing in the forefront of the revelation of Grace, the love of God, Father, Son, and Holy Spirit, to sinners of mankind, manifested especially in the Father's gift of the Son to be the Saviour of the world, in the coming of the Son to offer Himself a propitiation for sin, and in the striving of the Holy Spirit with men to bring them to repentance.

That this Church also holds that all who hear the Gospel are warranted and required to believe to the saving of their souls; and that in the case of such as do not believe, but perish in their sins, the issue is due to their own rejection of the Gospel call. That this Church does not teach, and does not regard the Confession as teaching, the fore-ordination of men to death irrespective of their own sin.

That it is the duty of those who believe, and one end of their calling by God, to make known the Gospel to all men everywhere for the obedience of faith. And that while the Gospel is the ordinary means of salvation for those to whom it is made known, yet it does not follow, nor is the Confession to be held as teaching, that any who died in infancy are lost, or that God may not extend His mercy, for Christ's sake, and by His Holy Spirit, to those who are beyond the reach of these means, as it may seem good to Him, according to the riches of His grace.

That, in holding and teaching, according to the Confession of Faith, the corruption of man's whole nature as fallen, this Church also maintains that there remain tokens of his greatness as created in the image of God; that he possesses a knowledge of God and of duty; that he is responsible for compliance with the moral law and with the Gospel; and that, although unable without the aid of the Holy Spirit to return to God, he is yet capable of affections and actions which in themselves are virtuous and praiseworthy.

That this Church disclaims intolerant or persecuting principles, and does not consider her office-bearers, in subscribing the Confession, committed to any principles inconsistent with liberty of conscience and the right of private judgment.

That while diversity of opinion is recognised in this Church on such points in the Confession as do not enter into the substance of the Reformed Faith therein set forth, the Church retains full authority to determine, in any case which may arise, what points fall within this description, and thus to guard against any abuse of this liberty to the detriment of sound doctrine, or to the injury of her unity and peace.

The Church of Scotland Act, 1921

An Act to declare the lawfulness of certain Articles declaratory of the Constitution of the Church of Scotland in matters spiritual prepared with the authority of the General Assembly of the Church.

[*28th July 1921*]

Whereas certain articles declaratory of the constitution of the Church of Scotland in matters spiritual have been prepared with the authority of the General Assembly of the Church, with a view to facilitate the union of other Churches with the Church of Scotland, which articles are set out in the Schedule to this Act, and together with any modifications of the said articles or additions thereto made in accordance therewith are hereinafter in this Act referred to as 'the Declaratory Articles':

And whereas it is expedient that any doubts as to the lawfulness of the Declaratory Articles should be removed:

Be it therefore enacted by the King's most Excellent Majesty, by and with the advice and consent of the Lords Spiritual and Temporal, and Commons, in this present Parliament assembled, and by the authority of the same, as follows:

1. The Declaratory Articles are lawful articles, and the constitution of the Church of Scotland in matters spiritual is as therein set forth, and no limitation of the liberty, rights, and powers in matters spiritual therein set forth shall be derived from any statute or law affecting the Church of Scotland in matters

spiritual at present in force, it being hereby declared that in all questions of construction the Declaratory Articles shall prevail, and that all such statutes and laws shall be construed in conformity. therewith and in subordination thereto, and all such statutes and laws in so far as they are inconsistent with the Declaratory Articles are hereby repealed and declared to be of no effect.

2. Nothing contained in this Act or in any other Act affecting the Church of Scotland shall prejudice the recognition of any other Church in Scotland as a Christian Church protected by law in the exercise of its spiritual functions.

3. Subject to the recognition of the matters dealt with in the Declaratory Articles as matters spiritual, nothing in this Act contained shall affect or prejudice the jurisdiction of the civil courts in relation to any matter of a civil nature.

4. This Act may be cited as the Church of Scotland Act, 1921, and shall come into operation on such date as His Majesty may fix by Order in Council after the Declaratory Articles shall have been adopted by an Act of the General Assembly of the Church of Scotland with the consent of a majority of the Presbyteries of the Church.

Articles Declaratory of the Constitution of the Church of Scotland in Matters Spiritual, 1926

I. The Church of Scotland is part of the Holy Catholic or Universal Church; worshipping one God, Almighty, all-wise, and all-loving, in the Trinity of the Father, the Son, and the Holy Ghost, the same in substance, equal in power and glory; adoring the Father, infinite in Majesty, of whom are all things; confessing our Lord Jesus Christ, the Eternal Son, made very man for our salvation; glorying in His Cross and Resurrection, and owning obedience to Him as the Head over all things to His Church; trusting in the promised renewal and guidance of the Holy Spirit; proclaiming the forgiveness of sins and acceptance with God through faith in Christ, and the gift of Eternal life; and labouring for the advancement of the Kingdom of God throughout the world. The Church of Scotland adheres to the Scottish Reformation; receives the Word of God which is contained in the

Scriptures of the Old and New Testaments as its supreme rule of faith and life; and avows the fundamental doctrines of the Catholic faith founded thereupon.

II. The principal subordinate standard of the Church of Scotland is the Westminster Confession of Faith approved by the General Assembly of 1647, containing the sum and substance of the Faith of the Reformed Church. Its government is Presbyterian, and is exercised through Kirk Sessions, Presbyteries, Provincial Synods, and General Assemblies. Its system and principles of worship, orders, and discipline are in accordance with 'The Directory for the Public Worship of God', 'The Form of Presbyterial Church Government', and 'The Form of Process', as these have been or may hereafter be interpreted or modified by Acts of the General Assembly or by consuetude.

III. This Church is in historical continuity with the Church of Scotland which was reformed in 1560, whose liberties were ratified in 1592, and for whose security provision was made in the Treaty of Union of 1707. The continuity and identity of the Church of Scotland are not prejudiced by the adoption of these Articles. As a national Church representative of the Christian Faith of the Scottish people it acknowledges its distinctive call and duty to bring the ordinances of religion to the people in every parish of Scotland through a territorial ministry.

IV. This Church, as part of the Universal Church wherein the Lord Jesus Christ has appointed a government in the hands of Church office-bearers, receives from Him, its Divine King and Head, and from Him alone, the right and power subject to no civil authority to legislate, and to adjudicate finally, in all matters of doctrine, worship, government, and discipline in the Church, including the right to determine all questions concerning membership and office in the Church, the constitution and membership of its Courts, and the mode of election of its office-bearers, and to define the boundaries of the spheres of labour of its ministers and other office-bearers. Recognition by civil authority of the separate and independent government and jurisdiction of this Church in matters spiritual, in whatever manner such recognition be expressed, does not in any way affect the character of this government and jurisdiction as derived from the Divine Head of the Church alone, or give to the civil authority any right of interference with the proceedings or judgments of the Church within the sphere of its spiritual government and jurisdiction.

V. This Church has the inherent right, free from interference by civil authority, but under the safeguards for deliberate action and legislation provided by the Church itself, to frame or adopt its subordinate standards, to declare the sense in which it understands its Confession of Faith, to modify the forms of expression therein, or to formulate other doctrinal statements, and to define the relation thereto of its office-bearers and members, but always in agreement with the Word of God and the fundamental doctrines of the Christian Faith contained in the said Confession, of which agreement the Church shall be sole judge, and with due regard to liberty of opinion in points which do not enter into the substance of the Faith.

VI. This Church acknowledges the divine appointment and authority of the civil magistrate within his own sphere, and maintains its historic testimony to the duty of the nation acting in its corporate capacity to render homage to God, to acknowledge the Lord Jesus Christ to be King over the nations, to obey His laws, to reverence His ordinances, to honour His Church, and to promote in all appropriate ways the Kingdom of God. The Church and the State owe mutual duties to each other, and acting within their respective spheres may signally promote each other's welfare. The Church and the State have the right to determine each for itself all questions concerning the extent and the continuance of their mutual relations in the discharge of these duties and the obligations arising therefrom.

VII. The Church of Scotland, believing it to be the will of Christ that His disciples should be all one in the Father and in Him, that the world may believe that the Father has sent Him, recognises the obligation to seek and promote union with other Churches in which it finds the Word to be purely preached, the sacraments administered according to Christ's ordinance, and discipline rightly exercised; and it has the right to unite with any such Church without loss of its identity on terms which this Church finds to be consistent with these Articles.

VIII. The Church has the right to interpret these Articles, and, subject to the safeguards for deliberate action and legislation provided by the Church itself, to modify or add to them; but always consistently with the provisions of the first Article hereof, adherence to which, as interpreted by the Church, is essential to its continuity and corporate life. Any proposal for a modification of or addition to these Articles which may be approved of by the General Assembly shall, before it can be enacted by the Assembly, be transmitted by way of overture to Presbyteries in at least two immediately successive years. If the overture shall receive the approval, with or without suggested amendment, of two-thirds of the whole of the Presbyteries of the Church, the Assembly may revise the overture in the light of any suggestions by Presbyteries, and may transmit the overture when so revised to Presbyteries for their consent. If the overture as transmitted in its final form shall receive the consent of not less than two-thirds of the whole of the Presbyteries of the Church, the General Assembly may, if it deems it expedient, modify or add to these Articles in terms of the said overture. But if the overture as transmitted in its final form shall not receive the requisite consent, the same or a similar proposal shall not be again transmitted for the consent of Presbyteries until an interval of five years after the failure to obtain the requisite consent has been reported to the General Assembly.

IX.   Subject to the provisions of the foregoing Articles and the powers of amendment therein contained, the Constitution of the Church of Scotland in matters spiritual is hereby anew ratified and confirmed by the Church.

Excerpts from the Preamble, Questions, and Formula prescribed in the 1929 Basis and Plan of Union for the Ordination and Induction of Ministers

... In this act of ordination the Church of Scotland, as part of the Holy Catholic or Universal Church worshipping One God — Father, Son, and Holy Spirit — affirms anew its belief in the Gospel of the sovereign grace and love of God, wherein through Jesus Christ, His only Son, our Lord, Incarnate, Crucified, and Risen, He freely offers to all men, upon repentance and faith, the forgiveness of sins, renewal by the Holy Spirit, and eternal life, and calls them to labour in the fellowship of faith for the advancement of the Kingdom of God throughout the world.

The Church of Scotland acknowledges the Word of God which is contained in the Scriptures of the Old and New Testaments to be the supreme rule of faith and life.

The Church of Scotland holds as its subordinate standard the Westminster Confession of Faith, recognising liberty of opinion on such points of doctrine as do not enter into the substance of the Faith, and claiming the right, in dependence on the promised guidance of the Holy Spirit, to formulate, interpret, or modify its subordinate standards: always in agreement with the fundamental doctrines of the Christian Faith contained in the said Confession — of which agreement the Church itself shall be sole judge.

(The Moderator then puts eight questions to the Ordinand or Minister to be inducted. The first three run as follows.)

1.   Do you believe in one God — Father, Son, and Holy Spirit; and do you confess anew the Lord Jesus Christ as your Saviour and Lord?

2.   Do you believe the Word of God, which is contained in the Scriptures of the Old and New Testaments, to be the supreme rule of faith and life?

3.   Do you believe the fundamental doctrines of the Christian faith contained in the Confession of Faith of this Church?

(After the questions have been satisfactorily answered, the Formula is signed.)

FORMULA

I believe the fundamental doctrines of the Christian faith contained in the Confession of Faith of this Church.

I acknowledge the Presbyterian government of this Church to be agreeable to the Word of God, and promise that I will submit thereunto and concur therewith.

I promise to observe the order of worship and the administration of all public ordinances as the same are or may be allowed in this Church.

(This same Formula is also signed by Elders on their admission to office.)

SELECT BIBLIOGRAPHY

1. General Works on Scottish Church History and Theology

BURLEIGH, J. H. S. *A Church History of Scotland*. London: O.U.P., 1960

DRUMMOND, A. L. and BULLOCH, J. *The Scottish Church 1688–1843*. Edinburgh: The Saint Andrew Press, 1973;
The Church in Victorian Scotland 1843–1874. Edinburgh: The Saint Andrew Press, 1975;
The Church in Late Victorian Scotland 1874–1900. Edinburgh: The Saint Andrew Press, 1978

HENDERSON, G. D. *The Burning Bush*. Studies in Scottish Church History. Edinburgh: The Saint Andrew Press, 1957

McCRIE, C. G. *The Confessions of the Church of Scotland*. Edinburgh: Macniven & Wallace, 1907

MACLEOD, J. *Scottish Theology in Relation to Church History Since the Reformation*. Repr. Edinburgh: Knox Press, 1974

2. Church Law and Subscription

COOPER, J. *Confessions of Faith and Formulas of Subscription ... especially in the Church of Scotland*. Glasgow: Maclehose, 1907

COX, J. T. *Practice and Procedure in the Church of Scotland*. 6th edn by D. F. M. Macdonald. Edinburgh: Church of Scotland, 1976

INNES, A. T. *The Law of Creeds in Scotland*. 2nd edn. Edinburgh: Blackwood, 1902

LYALL, F. *Of Presbyters and Kings*. Church and State in the Law of Scotland. Aberdeen: A.U.P., 1980

3. Puritanism and Federal Theology

BREWARD, I. (ed.) *The Work of William Perkins*. Abingdon: Sutton Courtenay Press, 1970

BROWN, W. A. 'Covenant Theology'. Hastings' *Encyclopaedia of Religion and Ethics*, vol. IV. Edinburgh: T. & T. Clark, 1911, pp. 216–24

EMERSON, E. H. 'Calvin and Covenant Theology'. *Church History* 25 (1956), pp. 136–44

KENDALL, R. T. *Calvin and English Calvinism to 1649.* Oxford: O.U.P., 1979; Paperback, 1981

LYALL, F. 'Of Metaphors and Analogies. Legal Language and Covenant Theology'. *Scottish Journal of Theology* 32 (1979), pp. 1–17

MARSHALL, G. *Presbyteries and Profits.* Calvinism and the Development of Capitalism in Scotland, 1560–1707. Oxford: Clarendon, 1980

MØLLER, J. G. 'The Beginnings of Puritan Covenant Theology'. *Journal of Ecclesiastical History* 14 (1963), pp. 46–67

TORRANCE, J. B. 'Covenant or Contract? A Study of the Theological Background of Worship in Seventeenth Century Scotland'. *Scottish Journal of Theology* 23 (1970), pp. 51–76;
'The Covenant Concept in Scottish Theology and Politics and Its Legacy'. *Scottish Journal of Theology* 34 (1981), pp. 225–43

TRINTERUD, L. J. 'The Origins of Puritanism'. *Church History* 20 (1951), pp. 37–57

YULE, G. S. *Puritans in Politics.* The Religious Legislation of the Long Parliament in the Light of Puritan Theology and History. Abingdon: Sutton Courtenay Press, 1981

4. *The Westminster Assembly*

BEVERIDGE, W. *A Short History of the Westminster Assembly.* Edinburgh: T. & T. Clark, 1904

CAMPBELL, W. M. *The Triumph of Presbyterianism.* Edinburgh: The Saint Andrew Press, 1958

CARRUTHERS, S. W. *The Everyday Work of the Westminster Assembly.* Philadelphia: The Presbyterian Historical Society, 1943;
The Westminster Confession of Faith. Being an account of the preparation and printing of its seven leading editions ... Manchester: R. Aikman & Son, 1937

DE WITT, J. R. *Jus Divinum.* The Westminster Assembly and the Divine Right of Church Government. Kampen: Kok, 1969

LEITH, J. H. *Assembly at Westminster.* Reformed Theology in the Making. Atlanta: John Knox Press, 1973

MITCHELL, A. F. *The Westminster Assembly.* Its History and Standards. London: Nisbet, 1883

MITCHELL, A. F. and STRUTHERS, J. (eds) *Minutes of the Sessions of the Westminster Assembly of Divines.* Edinburgh: Blackwood, 1874

WARFIELD, B. B. 'The Westminster Assembly and Its Work'. *Princeton Theological Review* 6 (1908), pp. 177–210; 353–91

5. *The Theology of the Confession*

BRIGGS, C. A. *Whither?* A theological question for the times. Edinburgh: T. & T. Clark, 1889

HENDRY, G. S. *The Westminster Confession for Today.* London: S.C.M. Press, 1960

HODGE, A. A. *A Commentary on the Confession of Faith.* Edited by W. H. Goold. London: Nelson, 1870; repr. as *The Confession of Faith.* A

Handbook of Christian Doctrine Expounding the Westminster Confession. London: Banner of Truth, 1958; 1961

REID, J. K. S. 'Foundation Documents of the Faith: VII. The Westminster Confession'. *Expository Times* 91 (1980), pp. 195–9

ROGERS, J. *Scripture in the Westminster Confession.* Kampen: Kok, 1967

ROLSTON, H. *John Calvin versus the Westminster Confession.* Atlanta: John Knox Press, 1972

SHAW, R. *An Exposition of the Confession of Faith.* Edinburgh, 1845; repr. Glasgow: Blackie, 1877

In addition to the numerous printed editions of the Confession, mention should be made of a recent rendering into modern English: *The Westminster Confession of Faith. A New Edition.* Edited by D. Kelly, H. McClure and P. B. Rollinson. Greenwood, S.C.: Attic Press, 1979.

CONTRIBUTORS

IAN BREWARD: Professor of Church History and History of Doctrine, Knox College, Dunedin, since 1965. From 1982 Professor of Church History, Ormond College, Melbourne. Moderator of the General Assembly of the Presbyterian Church in New Zealand, 1975. Publications include *The Work of William Perkins* and *Grace and Truth*.

ALEXANDER C. CHEYNE: Professor of Ecclesiastical History, University of Edinburgh, since 1964. Chalmers Lecturer, Glasgow and Aberdeen, 1976. Publications include articles and reviews in various journals and the Introduction to the reprint of Tulloch's *Movements of Religious Thought*.

GEORGE M. DALE: Now retired after ministries in four parishes, lastly in Dull and Weem, Perthshire. He is chairman of the National Church Association and editor of *The Reformed Book of Common Order*.

SINCLAIR B. FERGUSON: Associate minister at St George's-Tron, Glasgow, he received his doctorate for research in the theology of John Owen (1616–1683). An editorial adviser for the *Evangelical Quarterly*, he has written several books, including *Add to Your Faith* and *The Christian Life*.

ALASDAIR I. C. HERON: Professor of Reformed Theology in the University of Erlangen. Editor of *The Scottish Journal of Theology*. Publications include *Two Churches, One Love: Interchurch Marriage between Protestants and Roman Catholics* and *A Century of Protestant Theology*.

JOHN H. LEITH: Professor of Theology in Union Seminary, Richmond, Virginia. His books include *An Introduction to the Reformed Tradition* and *Assembly at Westminster*.

153

FRANCIS LYALL: Professor of Public Law in the University of Aberdeen since 1974, and an elder of the Church of Scotland. Apart from numerous articles on legal and theological topics he has written *Of Presbyters and Kings, Church and State in the Law of Scotland.*

JAMES S. McEWEN: Emeritus Professor of Church History, Aberdeen University, and former Master of Christ's College. Publications include *The Faith of John Knox* and the article on Knox in the current *Encyclopedia Britannica.*

DOUGLAS M. MURRAY: Minister of Polwarth Parish Church, Edinburgh, and editor of *Liturgical Review.* He received his doctorate for research in nineteenth-century Scottish church history, and has published articles in *Liturgical Review* and *Records of the Scottish Church History Society.*

RODERICK PETTIGREW: Minister of Dalbeattie: Park with Kirkgunzeon since 1959, and since 1973 Secretary of the Panel on Doctrine.

JAMES PHILIP: Minister of Holyrood Abbey, Edinburgh, since 1958. He has written several biblical and theological studies, including *Christian Maturity, Christian Warfare and Armour* and *A Time to Build.*

JOHN K. S. REID: Professor of Systematic Theology, University of Aberdeen, 1961–1976 and a founding editor of *The Scottish Journal of Theology.* He has published translations of Calvin, Karl Barth and Oscar Cullman and is author of *The Authority of Scripture, Life in Christ,* etc.

JOHN M. ROSS: Now retired from the Civil Service, he served from 1952 to 1968 as Secretary and then Convener of the Presbyterian Church of England's Committee on Law and History. He is the author of various articles and pamphlets on theology and church history.

JOHN THOMPSON: Professor of Systematic Theology in Union Theological College, Belfast. Formerly editor of *Biblical Theology,* he has written articles in several journals as well as *Christ in Perspective in the Theology of Karl Barth.*

JAMES B. TORRANCE: Professor of Systematic Theology, University of Aberdeen, since 1976. He has translated Oscar Cullmann and published several articles on the history of theology, with special concentration on Scottish Federal Theology.

GEORGE S. S. YULE: Professor of Church History, University of Aberdeen; formerly Professor of Church History, Ormond College, Melbourne. Publications include *Puritans in Politics.*